Becoming AI Native

This engaging guide is designed to demystify artificial intelligence (AI) in the business world, no advanced maths degrees or robotic companions are necessary. It tackles everything from traditional AI to the exciting realm of Generative AI, clearly distinguishing between what is genuinely beneficial and what is merely hype, all while demonstrating how to leverage AI to address real-world business challenges.

The first half of the book serves as an essential playbook for businesses eager to understand AI's potential. It cuts through the jargon, illuminating what AI can achieve and showcasing how organisations are already harnessing it to save time, enhance efficiency, and secure a competitive advantage.

The second half introduces the concept of the "AI Native"—a future where AI is seamlessly integrated into business operations and daily life. This transformation opens thrilling opportunities, including new markets and creative work methods. It also prompts critical questions, like what happens when AI falters? The book carefully balances optimism with caution, offering insights that inspire thoughtful reflection.

Whether you're leading a team, launching a startup, or gearing up for a technology-driven career, this book equips readers to make informed decisions about AI. It is an essential resource for executives, entrepreneurs, and graduate students alike, stripping away the buzzwords to deliver actionable insights.

"This book brilliantly frames the evolution we're witnessing firsthand at micro1—where traditional recruiters are becoming AI Recruiter Operators, empowered not only to oversee but to strategically command powerful AI systems. Terence, Mark, Danny and Paul insightfully highlight this shift toward an 'AI native' world, underscoring how professionals are evolving from task-driven roles into strategic bosses of AI-driven workflows. Anyone looking to thrive, rather than just survive, in this AI-native era should read this essential guide."
Ali Ansar, *CEO, micro1.ai and Computer Science MS, Stanford University*

"Mastering the business of AI is no longer just a corporate goal, it is a cornerstone of our economic future—this book provides the blueprint."
Duncan Chiu, *Hong Kong Special Administrative Region Legislative Council Member (Technology and Innovation Constituency)*

"Insightful and action-oriented, this book bridges the gap between AI theory and real-world transformation—a must-read for executives who aim to lead with vision and agility."
Roger Spitz, *Futurist and Award-Winning Author; President, Techistential; Chair, Disruptive Futures Institute (San Francisco)*

"The transition to an 'AI Native' world is the defining challenge of our generation; *Becoming AI Native: Charting the Next AI Frontier* is the essential map for navigating it wisely."
Kary Bheemaiah, *Vice President, Chief Tech and Innovation Officer (CTIO), Capgemini Invent*

"*Becoming AI Native: Charting the Next AI Frontier* is like a crash course in smart digital leadership. It gives you a super practical game plan for going all-in on AI—perfect for any company that wants to crush it in the next wave of innovation."
Mark Schlesinger, *Former CIO, Broadridge*

"With AI now serving as the ultimate competitive edge, this book is an essential guide for leaders. It offers a road map to rethinking and transforming organizations for a smarter, more digital future."
Yih-Ray Hwang, *National Policy Advisor to the President of Taiwan*

"As artificial intelligence reshapes every facet of society, this book provides the strategic compass we urgently need. *Becoming AI Native: Charting the Next AI Frontier* distils complexity into actionable insight for leaders, thinkers, and builders of the AI era."
Amit Kapoor, *Chairman, Institute for Competitiveness*

"Excellent overview of the evolution of AI over the years and the pathways towards an AI native future. A forward-looking and practical framework for forward-thinking practitioners and senior executives to shape their organisation's digital transformation."
Maarten Kelder, *Former MD, Monitor Deloitte (Asia) and Temus (Temasek)*

"Forget AI road maps. This book quietly asks the essential: in becoming AI-native, what part of our nature are we rewiring and what does embracing AI mean for those who seek to lead amid the unpredictable human-driven evolution of intelligence itself."
Hamilton Mann, *Best-selling author of* Artificial Integrity *and originator of the concept of Artificial Integrity*

"*Becoming AI Native: Charting the Next AI Frontier* is a timely and indispensable guide for anyone seeking to understand and leverage the transformative power of artificial intelligence. The authors successfully bridge the gap between traditional AI and the emerging landscape of Generative AI, providing a practical and deeply informed roadmap for business leaders, technologists, and policymakers alike. What sets this book apart is its comprehensive approach—not only demystifying the technical foundations of AI but also exploring the strategic, societal, and ethical dimensions of becoming truly 'AI native.' From the solid grounding in rule-based systems and machine learning to the dynamic world of autonomous agentic AI, the authors provide a rare combination of clarity, foresight, and actionable insight. In a world increasingly shaped by algorithms and uncertainty, this book is both a compass and a call to action. It challenges readers to think beyond hype cycles and take ownership of AI's role in shaping our collective future. It is one of the must-reads for those ready to lead responsibly in the age of intelligence."
Makoto Shibata, *Head, Finolab*

"*Becoming AI Native: Charting the Next AI Frontier* captures the urgency and opportunity of this moment. It's a timely guide for leaders and organizations across the Asia-Pacific—and beyond—to turn AI potential into economic impact."
Dr Richard B. Dasher, *Director, US-Asia Technology Management Center, Stanford University*

"I highly recommended this excellent book, written lucidly by academia and practitioners, for AI novices like me who desire to be informed of the various AI technologies out there—their evolution, their abilities, and their limitations. At APS, we have developed with the assistance of Nexus FrontierTech an AI Fundamental ESG System, which has helped us make better investment decisions. I expect more AI solutions in our lives, business, etc. as the technology improves."
Wong Kok Hoi, *Founder and Chief Strategist, APS Asset Management*

"Artificial intelligence is not magic. Despite the incessant hyperbole, there are no shibboleths that turn water into wine or hay into gold. Yes, AI can be transformative to your business, but effective AI takes work: careful, disciplined engineering of the necessary infrastructure with well-governed data curation and then, and only then, the application of still-evolving AI algorithms. *Becoming AI Native: Charting the Next AI Frontier* does an excellent job of articulating this foundational truth. Terence, Mark, Danny and Paul lay out the history, the intellectual underpinnings, and, without apology, the difficult homework that makes the effective implementation of contemporary artificial intelligence possible. Any CEO who needs artificial intelligence in his business—which is all of us—should read this book before committing to a major investment. It will save him time and improve the likelihood that the AI he buys will generate the results he needs."
Stephen C. Daffron, *Co-Founder of Motive Partners and Chairman, BetaNXT*

"In an era where organisations are seeking clear guidance, *Becoming AI Native: Charting the Next AI Frontier* will prove as an indispensable guide for executives who are seeking to understand the benefits and pitfalls of AI and will use it to help navigate their organisations through an inevitable period of material change."
Ben Bacon, *Managing Director, Mitsubishi UFJ Financial Group*

Becoming AI Native

Charting the Next AI Frontier

Terence C. M. Tse, Mark Esposito,
Danny Goh and Paul Lee

CRC Press
Taylor & Francis Group
Boca Raton London New York

CRC Press is an imprint of the
Taylor & Francis Group, an **informa** business
A CHAPMAN & HALL BOOK

Designed cover image: Terence C.M. Tse, Mark Esposito, Danny Goh and Paul Lee

First edition published 2026
by CRC Press
2385 NW Executive Center Drive, Suite 320, Boca Raton FL 33431

and by CRC Press
4 Park Square, Milton Park, Abingdon, Oxon, OX14 4RN

CRC Press is an imprint of Taylor & Francis Group, LLC

ISBN: 978-1-032-90764-2 (hbk)
ISBN: 978-1-032-90763-5 (pbk)
ISBN: 978-1-003-55966-5 (ebk)

DOI: 10.1201/9781003559665

Typeset in Minion
by KnowledgeWorks Global Ltd.

To the next generation of pioneers—brilliant minds everywhere who refuse to accept the world as it is—with whom we will forge a new alliance between human wisdom and artificial intelligence, one that unlocks unprecedented possibilities for healing our planet, expanding human flourishing, and ensuring that no dream is too distant to reach.

Contents

Authors

Terence C.M. Tse is a Professor of Finance at Hult International Business School. He co-founded the AI Native Foundation and the Chart ThinkTank; Terence is also a co-founder and Executive Director of Nexus FrontierTech, an AI company. Furthermore, he is a Visiting Professor at both ESCP Business School and Cotrugli Business School.

Mark Esposito is a public policy scholar and social scientist affiliated with Harvard's Berkman Klein Center for Internet and Society and the Center for International Development at Harvard Kennedy School. He leads policy clinics on the governance of technology worldwide. He is a Professor at Hult International Business School and Adjunct Professor at Georgetown University. He has co-founded several AI ventures, including Nexus FrontierTech, the AI Native Foundation, and The Chart ThinkTank, and serves as Chief Economist at micro1, a Silicon Valley–based AI lab. He is a member of the World Economic Forum's Global AI Alliance, a Senior Advisor at Strategy& (PwC), a professorial fellow of the Mohammed Bin Rashid School of Government, and the co-author of 14 books.

Danny Goh is a serial entrepreneur, early stage investor, and AI pioneer. As Founder and CEO of Nexus FrontierTech, he leads an AI research lab transforming unstructured data into actionable insights for global enterprises and governments. Danny serves as an Entrepreneurship Expert at the Saïd Business School, Oxford University, and a Senior Fellow at École des Ponts Business School, Paris. He co-authored the bestseller *The AI Republic: Building the Nexus between Humans and Intelligent Automation* and co-founded the AI Native Foundation and the Chart ThinkTank, uniting experts and policymakers to accelerate AI transformation across industries.

Paul Lee is a tech entrepreneur dedicated to making sophisticated technology simple and accessible. His latest venture, Graiphene AI, empowers small businesses by automating complex workflows. Previously, he founded the award-winning Aumeo Audio for personalized sound and Vocofy.ai for AI voice preservation.

CHAPTER 1

Introduction

AT THE START OF *The AI Republic: Building the Nexus between Humans and Intelligent Automation*, published in 2019, we presented readers with a list of sentences, courtesy of the *Wall Street Journal*, to discern whether machines or humans had composed them. This exercise, intended to illustrate the rapid advancements in AI, often left readers astonished by the machines' capacity to imitate human-like writing. The results surprised many individuals. What was once deemed a challenging task for AI had become trivial. Today, the same test would yield no surprises, as AI technologies have progressed significantly along their development path. The lines between human- and machine-generated content have grown increasingly blurred, rendering it nearly impossible to differentiate between them. The technologies have become far more sophisticated, and our acceptance and expectations of them have increased. The tangible benefits and transformative potential of AI across various industries and aspects of our lives fuel this shift in perception. However, amidst this monumental progress, a pervasive confusion, if not outright misunderstanding, regarding the capabilities and limitations of AI persists. While AI can automate tasks, generate creative content, and even replicate human-like conversations, it still lacks proper understanding, consciousness, and the ability to reason abstractly. The introduction of Generative AI (GenAI) to the public in October 2022, through OpenAI's ChatGPT or Google's Gemini, has further complicated these issues. These powerful language models, capable of producing text of human quality, have ignited both excitement and apprehension, raising questions about the future of work, creativity, and the essence of intelligence.

DOI: 10.1201/9781003559665-1

Although GenAI is a direct extension of neural networks and deep learning, the fundamental blocks for earlier forms of AI, we observe that the development pathways in the business context differ. To create a conceptual separation, we will refer to the type of AI developed before GenAI as "traditional AI." Such distinction is essential regarding where each of these technologies can excel. In our experience, traditional AI is best used by companies to embed it to automate tasks. This typically involves processes that are repetitive, rule-based, and require high accuracy, such as data entry, fraud detection, or basic customer service interactions. Traditional AI excels in these scenarios because it can be trained on large datasets of structured data to identify patterns and make predictions with high accuracy. Granted, we are now, as retail customers, increasingly able to use (allegedly) AI-powered applications provided by various vendors. However, the capabilities of these applications are often limited to predefined functionalities determined and integrated by the vendor in their product and service offerings. This stands in contrast to GenAI, which, with its ability to generate novel content and adapt to a broader range of tasks, opens up possibilities for users to interact directly with and leverage AI capabilities in a more customised and dynamic way.

INDIVIDUAL USE OF GENAI IS BECOMING POPULAR

Everyone can use ChatGPT and Gemini or even DeepSeek for "free." These large language models (LLMs) are available for public use through web interfaces and Application Programming Interfaces (APIs), allowing individuals to experiment with and harness their capabilities without any upfront costs. Of course, many companies have made GenAI an integral part of their customer offerings—or have at least tried to. This includes integrating GenAI into existing products, such as Microsoft's incorporation of ChatGPT into its Bing search engine and creating entirely new services and applications powered by GenAI. However, this doesn't dispel the fact that individuals can access GenAI without any companies other than the GenAI suppliers themselves. Put it simply, while traditional AI is more of a wholesale technology, GenAI is a retail one. This fundamental difference in accessibility and distribution models significantly affects how GenAI is adopted and utilised across various sectors, potentially democratising access to advanced AI capabilities.

For the moment, let's focus on using GenAI in the workplace. If everyone can easily access GenAI, it is not difficult to imagine that many will incorporate it into their daily work routine. This widespread adoption is driven by the potential of GenAI to augment human capabilities, automate tasks, and enhance productivity across a wide range of professional activities. The latest studies have suggested that GenAI is already helping people to be more productive.

For instance, researchers found that, on average, people with the (GenAI-powered) Copilot for Microsoft 365 read 11% fewer individual emails and spent 4% less time interacting with them than people without Copilot.[1] This is attributable to these workers using the built-in summarise emails feature and the chat function, which enables them to retrieve information without having to read or reread individual emails. These findings highlight the tangible benefits of GenAI in streamlining communication and information access, freeing up time for more strategic and value-adding tasks. Another study of 758 consultants at BCG has shown that for each of 18 realistic consulting tasks that are accomplishable by AI, consultants using GenAI were significantly more productive and produced substantially higher-quality results. Consultants across the skills distribution benefited considerably from having AI augmentation, with those below the average performance threshold increasing by 43% and those above rising by 17% compared to their scores.[2] This demonstrates GenAI's potential to improve efficiency and elevate the overall quality of work output, even among highly skilled professionals.

BUSINESSES ARE STRUGGLING WITH TAKING ON AI

Small wonder many of us have rushed to embrace GenAI. Its accessibility and ease of use have empowered individuals to leverage its capabilities for various tasks, driving bottom-up adoption within organisations. Yet, while workers quickly involve GenAI in their daily work, their employers need help systematically and formally adopting AI technology. This disconnect between individual enthusiasm and organisational inertia highlights the challenges of integrating AI into existing workflows, processes, and corporate cultures. The truth is that many companies are struggling to incorporate traditional AI into their operations, not to mention GenAI. This difficulty stems from various factors, including a lack of clear strategy, insufficient technical expertise, data security and privacy concerns, ageing IT systems, and organisational resistance to change.

A recent survey by the US Census Bureau on how businesses have used AI can shed some light on AI adoption among companies.[3] Firstly, it finds that employees are faster than their companies when using AI, especially for large businesses and the information sector. This trend underscores

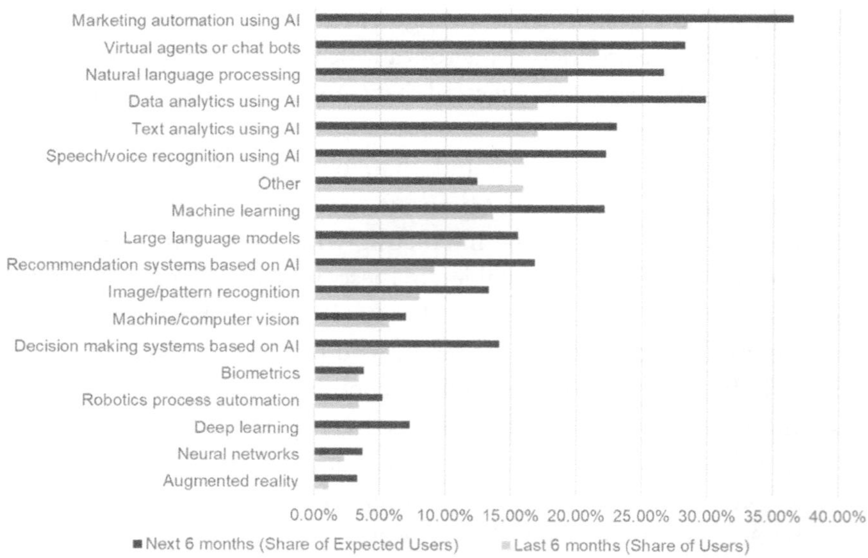

FIGURE 1.1 AI technologies or applications used by businesses.

the need for organisations to bridge this gap by providing clear guidelines, training programmes, and supportive infrastructure to facilitate AI adoption. Secondly, **Figure 1.1** shows the applications the respondents have used AI for. While the specific applications mentioned in the figure are not detailed here, the overall trend reveals a focus on tasks that are easily automated or augmented by current AI capabilities. It can be seen that while they are all keen to expand their use of AI in the next six months, the most popular applications involved are writing, image and video creation, automated marketing, and processing information. The problem is that these are relatively low-added activities. This emphasis on low-hanging fruit suggests that many companies are still in the early stages of AI adoption, focusing on incremental improvements rather than transformative changes. Thirdly, the survey reveals that the most common reason, cited by 81% of the businesses not expecting to use AI, is that AI does not apply to them. This suggests that many companies may not yet foresee a need for, or a benefit from, AI. This *perception* gap could be attributed to a lack of understanding of AI's potential applications or a mismatch between current AI capabilities and the specific needs of their industry. As the second most prevalent barrier, over 7% of companies indicated a lack of knowledge of the capabilities of AI. Indeed, small and medium-sized businesses often lack the financial resources or technical skills to use AI.

This *resource* gap further reinforces the need for educational initiatives and industry-wide efforts to demystify AI and showcase its potential value across various sectors.

These findings don't surprise us—they are similar to what we can see in our front-row seats providing AI solutions to companies worldwide. As practitioners working directly with businesses on their AI journeys, we have witnessed firsthand the challenges and complexities companies face in adopting and integrating AI into their operations. This view, however, seems to contradict what academic and media circles have been portraying directly. The prevailing narrative in scholarly research and popular media often focuses on the transformative potential of AI, highlighting successful case studies and emphasising the technology's rapid advancements. If such reporting on AI is taken at face value, far more businesses would have already reaped the benefits from their extensive use of AI technologies to run their operations. This discrepancy between the reality on the ground and the optimistic portrayals in the media may result from several factors. Firstly, there is often a (long) time lag between developing cutting-edge AI technologies and their widespread adoption by businesses. Secondly, media coverage tends to focus on shiny objects and attention-grabbing stories, under-representing the company's experience with AI on average. Thirdly, there may be a tendency to overestimate the maturity and capabilities of current AI technologies, leading to unrealistic expectations about their immediate impact. What separates hype from reality can create confusion and scepticism among business leaders, hindering the responsible and effective adoption of AI.

We must move beyond headlines and cut through the cacophony. This is partially what we aim to achieve with this book. We want to provide a more realistic and accurate view of AI, cutting through the hype and sensationalism that often dominate media coverage. Given the widespread interest and attention in AI technology, it's sometimes difficult to believe that so few books have been written on the business of AI. This book could somewhat bridge the knowledge gap. More specifically, there are three objectives:

Objective 1: Demystifying Traditional AI for Business Adoption

We want to offer a concise yet comprehensive review of how traditional AI operates, emphasising why the only way for companies to integrate effectively is to commit substantial time, resources, and effort. Even though it has been almost a decade since traditional AI was introduced to businesses, many companies—like those responding to the survey mentioned above—are still wondering how to capitalise on this increasingly mature technology. We will in this book provide actionable insights for entrepreneurs, managers, and executives seeking to introduce AI into their businesses successfully.

Objective 2: Navigating the Evolving Landscape of GenAI

The latter chapters provide an accessible explanation of how GenAI functions and insights into how companies have been and could be deploying it. From our client engagements, we have started to see a growing trend of companies exploring and experimenting with GenAI applications across various domains. Real-world case studies, best practices, and practical guidance are provided for companies seeking to harness the power of GenAI while navigating its ethical and societal implications.

Objective 3: Envisioning the Future of AI: The Rise of the AI Native

We not only want to look at the past and the present, but also to peek into what lies ahead of us, delving into the broader ramifications of AI technology and exploring its societal and individual implications in the years to come. It introduces the concept of "AI native," wherein AI becomes integral to our day-to-day functioning, be it for companies or individuals, fundamentally altering the economic and social dynamics like what smartphones and the Internet have done to us in the past.

The book is divided into two parts, each containing several chapters, to achieve these three objectives. Part 1 primarily focuses on AI technologies and their business applications, addressing objectives 1 and 2. Part 2, however, takes a further step to examine how AI technologies might perform in the distant future, outlining the business, economic, and social implications in line with objective 3.

PART 1

In chapter 2, titled "Traditional AI: Taking Advantage of a Proven Technology," we offer an in-depth exploration of the intricate technical foundations of traditional AI, discussing the evolution from rule-based algorithms to machine learning and deep learning. These concepts were first introduced and elucidated in *The AI Republic: Building the Nexus between Humans and Intelligent Automation*. The chapter mirrors the successful approach employed in our previous book, which aimed to demystify AI for a broad audience ranging from professionals to graduate school students. It seeks to empower our readers with a comprehensive understanding of AI's technical underpinnings. Beyond simply explaining the "what" of traditional AI, this chapter delves into the "how," providing a clear and accessible explanation of the underlying algorithms, techniques, and data structures that power these systems. This foundational knowledge will enable readers to move beyond a superficial understanding of AI and engage with its capabilities and limitations more critically.

Chapter 3 is titled "Traditional AI in Current Business Use." As suggested, the goal here is to provide a detailed account of our firsthand experiences developing AI capabilities for our clients worldwide. By distilling lessons from our client engagements, we illustrate how businesses harnessed AI to gain a competitive edge. Moreover, we showcase the tangible benefits derived from the strategic implementation of AI solutions across various industries and sectors. It serves as a practical guide, offering insights into the essential steps and best practices for initiating and executing AI projects. We aim to equip readers with the knowledge and tools necessary to embark on their AI journey confidently and effectively.

Chapter 4 channels the attention to what GenAI can do and how to harness it. This unexpected offspring of AI technology undoubtedly represents a groundbreaking change. In stark contrast to traditional AI, which primarily focuses on recognising patterns within existing datasets to make predictions or classifications, GenAI delves deeper into understanding the fundamental structure of the data itself, developing the capability to create something new. This new way of working has opened up new possibilities for all of us and potentially many value-creating business opportunities. This chapter seeks to provide a comprehensive and accessible introduction to GenAI, explaining its underlying principles, capabilities, and limitations. We attempt to "make easy" complex technical concepts, using clear language and illustrative examples to make this cutting-edge technology understandable for a broad audience. Moreover, by double-clicking the inner workings of GenAI, we unveil the intricate algorithms and techniques that underpin its remarkable capabilities, offering you a nuanced understanding of its potential applications and limitations.

Chapter 5, "Current and Future Trajectories of GenAI," explores the evolving landscape of generative artificial intelligence, tracing its rapid post-ChatGPT rise and the sweeping transformations it's triggering across industries. The chapter examines how GenAI is reshaping productivity, displacing specific jobs, and redefining competitive advantage—yet also grapples with practical challenges, such as data scarcity, hardware bottlenecks, and sustainability concerns. It maps the GenAI value chain, demystifies foundation models, and walks through the three main adoption strategies—prompt engineering, retrieval-augmented generation, and fine-tuning—each offering a laddered path to business integration. The chapter also highlights the paradox of GenAI's hype versus its slower-than-expected enterprise uptake, attributing the "use case crisis" to historical patterns of tech diffusion and the need for an evolved ecosystem. It sets the stage for understanding why GenAI is both irresistibly promising and maddeningly complex.

The chapter that follows, "GenAI in Current Business Use," dives into the often-surprising realities of deploying GenAI in the trenches of business. Despite the hype and accessible tools, the chapter reveals a persistent disconnect between promise and performance—where even well-resourced firms stumble over hallucinating chatbots, unclear ROI, legacy systems, and talent shortages. Drawing from client stories and industry data, the chapter unpacks why GenAI success requires far more than fancy models: strong management, robust data infrastructure, human-AI collaboration, and tailored solutions—especially for small and mid-sized enterprises. Through practical frameworks like the "AI Factory" and real-world use cases, the chapter highlights how value can be unlocked if businesses go beyond productivity plays and systematically integrate GenAI into operations. In short, GenAI may "talk" well, but thinking straight in a business context? That still takes a village—and a plan.

PART 2

Part 2 propels us into AI's broader societal and individual implications, moving beyond business applications to explore how this transformative technology will reshape our lives. We envision a future where AI becomes ubiquitous and seamlessly integrated into our daily routines and decision-making processes, giving rise to what we term the "AI native." This section examines the exciting possibilities and potential challenges of this AI-driven future, encouraging readers to engage with this technological revolution's ethical, social, and economic implications.

As we show in Chapter 7, "AI Native," the rise of AI agents will potentially change the nature of business, including how they could favour incumbents and reduce management layers (and staff). In this impending future, AI will no longer be confined to business. Analogous to the transformative impact of smartphones on personal communication, the proliferation of AI "apps" will fundamentally alter the dynamics of consumer decision-making, empowering individuals to make informed choices in real time. This is particularly true when non-business users can "harness the power of agentic AI."

As we entrust AI with ever-greater responsibilities, we must grapple with the unintended consequences of this delegation. As the chapter title suggests, we argue Chapter 8 that we cannot leave AI unchecked. It moves beyond the often-discussed ethical concerns surrounding AI, such as job displacement and privacy violations, to delve into more nuanced and under-explored issues. We challenge readers to consider the potential long-term consequences of unchecked AI development on our values, beliefs, and societal structures. We also ask how AI may lead to the atrophy of critical thinking skills as we increasingly rely on automated solutions, deskilling us and even dumbing us down, turning on our autopilot to follow algorithm-issued instructions without questioning them. These are important considerations as we edge towards the era of AI native. By raising these challenging questions, we aim to stimulate critical reflection and dialogue around AI's societal impact, emphasising the need for proactive and ethical decision-making to shape a future where AI empowers rather than endangers humanity.

The last chapter reminds us that discussing AI's future is to venture into the unknown. What is not unknown is that businesses and societies are at the cusp of a step change shaped and driven by AI.

Amidst these complexities and uncertainties, the question arises: Will our world be fundamentally better or worse off due to AI's ascent? The answer remains to be discovered. It will be a product of our collective choices and actions in the years to come. It is up to us to decide.

We sincerely hope this book will help you find the right way forward.

NOTES

1 Jaffe, Sonia et al. (2024) "Generative AI in real-world workplaces," *Microsoft Research*, July 29, https://www.microsoft.com/en-us/research/publication/generative-ai-in-real-world-workplaces/. Accessed on 19 August 2024.

2 Dell'Acqua, Fabrizio et al. (2023) "Navigating the jagged technological frontier: Field experimental evidence of the effects of AI on knowledge worker productivity and quality," *Harvard Business School Working Paper*, 24-013, https://www.hbs.edu/ris/Publication%20Files/24-013_d9b45b68-9e74-42d6-a1c6-c72fb70c7282.pdf. Accessed on 19 August 2024.
3 Bonney, Katherine et al. (2024) "Tracking firm use of AI in real time: A snapshot from the Business Trends and Outlook Survey," *US Census Bureau*, CES 24-16, March, https://www.census.gov/hfp/btos/downloads/CES-WP-24-16.pdf. Accessed on 16 August 2024.

CHAPTER 2

Traditional AI

Taking Advantage of a Proven Technology

In the ever-evolving landscape of AI, keeping pace with developments can often feel like following an intricate television series with myriad intertwining plotlines and character relationships. As you begin to grasp one new twist, you struggle to recall the past connections that led to this point. This sensation of constant flux and revelation is particularly pronounced in the current era, where media outlets bombard us daily with the latest breakthroughs and developments in Generative AI (GenAI). The twists and turns of the storyline of GenAI in season two make it easy for us to forget the drama and intricate relationships of the previous generations of AI featured in season one. The ubiquity of GenAI in contemporary discourse has created an intriguing phenomenon: for many, GenAI has become synonymous with AI itself. While understandable, given the technology's prominence, this perception overlooks the rich tapestry of AI's history and the multitude of approaches that fall under its broad umbrella. To truly appreciate the current state of AI and its potential future trajectories, we must first revisit the foundations upon which these cutting-edge technologies are built.

In his research, Terence has examined the factors that propel a single invention or innovation into hype. One frequently observed catalyst that often generates technology bubbles is when retail customers—individuals like you and me—have easy access to them. Public imagination can run

DOI: 10.1201/9781003559665-2

wild when we can see, touch, and feel a piece of new technology. For instance, people who interact with ChatGPT may extrapolate their experience to encompass the entire field of AI, assuming that all AI systems possess the same capabilities and limitations. This can lead to unrealistic expectations and a distorted understanding of the field's true potential. We are certainly not dismissing GenAI as mere hype or a bubble; its potential and impact are undeniable. However, the fervour surrounding GenAI raises essential questions about its future trajectories and its place within the broader AI landscape. Will it live up to its transformative promises or fade into the background like other hyped technologies? Will it reshape industries as many predict or primarily serve as a supplementary tool within existing workflows?

These questions require nuanced and multifaceted analysis, moving beyond the hype to understand GenAI's capabilities and limitations. This includes examining critical issues such as the propensity for AI systems to produce inaccurate or misleading outputs, often termed "hallucinations," and the potential for malicious actors to exploit AI for nefarious purposes, sometimes referred to as "botshit" in Mark's research. While focusing on the drivers of technological adoption, Terence's research intersects with a broader conversation on the governance of AI, a theme explored in Mark's work. Mark's research delves into AI's wider societal and policy implications, examining how this technology impacts our lives beyond business and technology. His work grapples with the ethical considerations of AI, questioning its potential impact on employment, privacy, and even the fabric of our social interactions. The intersection of these two research strands underscores a crucial point: understanding AI requires a multidisciplinary approach. It demands that we consider the technical advancements and their social, economic, and ethical implications. As we navigate the evolving landscape of AI, it is imperative to combine the insights of researchers like Terence and Mark, bridging the gap between technological innovation and its impact on individuals and society. We will explore these questions in greater depth later in this book.

Amidst this excitement and uncertainty, many companies grapple with a fundamental question: If the path forward with GenAI is unclear, what can be done with AI in the meantime? This is where what we term "traditional AI" comes into play—the established, proven AI technologies that have revolutionised industries for years at the backend of different businesses instead of the customer-facing side. In this chapter, we will revisit the critical characteristics of these "older" forms of AI that many companies have already implemented or are poised to utilise. We will revisit the past plotlines within our metaphorical TV series, offering a more comprehensive and thoughtful "previously on" segment to contextualise, if not make sense of, the current developments. The following chapter will then delve deeper into real-world applications, examining how companies use AI in their operations. By understanding traditional AI's historical context and current applications, we can better appreciate the full spectrum of AI technologies and their potential impact on business and society.

Traditional AI encompasses various techniques, often categorised into symbolic AI, statistical AI, and a hybrid. Symbolic AI or rule-based AI, prominent in the early days, relies on explicit rules and logical reasoning to solve problems. Think of it as programming a computer with a detailed instruction manual for every scenario. Conversely, statistical AI, including machine learning, uses data and statistical models to enable machines to learn patterns and make predictions. Effectively, this feeds a vast dataset to a computer and lets it figure out the underlying relationships. This approach has gained significant traction in recent years due to the increasing availability of data and computational power.

The distinction between GenAI and traditional AI also lies in their objectives and capabilities. Traditional AI excels at specific tasks such as image classification, fraud detection, or recommendation systems. These AI systems are often trained on big data to identify patterns and make predictions within a narrowly defined scope. They operate within a set of pre-defined rules or learn to make decisions based on the data they are fed, but their output is generally predictable and aligned with the task they were designed to perform. GenAI, however, aims to create something new. It focuses on generating content, ranging from text and code to images and music, often blurring the lines between human and machine creativity. Instead of merely analysing or acting upon existing data, GenAI takes a set of inputs and uses them to generate entirely new and original outputs. This ability to create stems from its training on massive and diverse datasets, encompassing text, code, images, audio, and more. This broad exposure enables GenAI to learn the underlying patterns and structures of different forms of content, allowing it to generate outputs that are often indistinguishable from human-created content.

This difference in objectives translates to a variation in potential applications. While traditional AI excels at automating tasks and enhancing efficiency, GenAI unveils exciting new possibilities in creative industries, research, and beyond. For instance, GenAI can assist writers in overcoming writer's block, aid artists in generating original visual concepts, or hasten scientific discovery by developing hypotheses and simulating experiments. However, this capacity to create novel content also raises concerns about potential misuse, such as the creation of deepfakes, the dissemination of misinformation, and the possible displacement of human creativity across various fields. Navigating these ethical and societal implications will be crucial as GenAI continues to evolve and permeate our lives. Nevertheless, traditional AI shouldn't be perceived as merely a stepping stone on the path to GenAI. While GenAI captures the limelight, traditional AI provides immense value across numerous applications. Its proven track record in areas like predictive maintenance, fraud detection, document extraction, and personalised marketing showcases its capacity to drive efficiency, reduce costs, and enhance customer experiences. Businesses that embrace traditional AI can unlock significant benefits today while simultaneously positioning themselves for the future evolution of AI. Furthermore, the future of AI might not represent a dichotomy but rather a synergy between traditional AI and GenAI. Envision a world where GenAI interacts with customers and addresses their queries while traditional AI analyses and refines them for optimal results. Traditional AI's strength in structured data analysis could complement GenAI's creative potential, leading to even more powerful and innovative applications. By combining the strengths of both approaches, we can unlock new possibilities and propel further advancements in AI.

THE ABC OF AI

In Lewis Carroll's masterpiece, "Alice's Adventures in Wonderland," we find advice that, while seemingly simple, carries profound wisdom: "Begin at the beginning and go on till you come to the end: then stop." This guidance, when applied to the realm of AI, offers two valuable insights. Firstly, it suggests that progress is often non-linear. The development of AI technologies has been marked by fits and starts, breakthroughs and setbacks, rather than a straightforward path from conception to realisation. Secondly, it underscores the importance of building upon a solid foundation, systematically proceeding step by step with caution until reaching the desired outcome. Developing and implementing AI technologies in business operations aligns with these principles. To truly understand AI as we know it today, we must recognise that it has evolved significantly from its initial conception. The term "AI" emerged in 1956 at the Dartmouth Conference, a gathering of academics from various disciplines to explore ways for machines to mimic human intelligence. However, this early vision was more of a thought experiment than a practical roadmap for building human-like machines.

When we consider how to build AI, many of us instinctively think of programming machines to respond in specific ways to particular conditions or criteria. In essence, this approach is an elaborate version of the "if-then" statements familiar to users of spreadsheet software. Initially, this rule-based, symbolic approach seemed promising and set the course for early AI development. However, over time, the limitations of this method became increasingly apparent. One major constraint is the complexity of defining rules for every possible scenario. Programmers face the daunting task of compiling a complete list of rules to ensure an algorithm works appropriately in all situations. Sure, it is possible to flush out all the rules in some circumstances. If a customer enters all the data needed on your shop's web page, the customer can proceed to the following page. However, how can you build a chatbot that can tackle and respond reasonably to *all* potential customer queries? Even if you manage to get 80% right, it is still far from helpful. This challenge is analogous to learning a new language—even mastering 80% of the grammar will still result in numerous errors in real-world usage. Moreover, while diligent effort might address the "known unknowns," it is virtually impossible to anticipate every "unknown unknown"—those situations and variables we can't conceive of until we encounter them. This effectively restricts our ability to assemble a list of all the rules necessary. This limitation is further compounded by what philosopher Michael Polanyi termed the "Polanyi Paradox": the phenomenon where we intuitively understand how to perform specific tasks but cannot verbalise the rules or procedures governing them. In many aspects of our lives, we rely on tacit knowledge—from driving a car to riding a bicycle to engaging in creative pursuits. These activities, which we perform relatively quickly, are challenging to express verbally or translate into explicit rules for a machine to follow. Consider, for instance, the seemingly simple task of recognising one's parents. A three-year-old child can do this effortlessly, but programming a machine to perform the same feat with comparable accuracy and nuance is extraordinarily challenging. Just try to describe what your parents look like.

As these limitations accumulated, it became evident that such a deterministic, rule-based approach to AI had reached its limit. Like a ball striking a ceiling, there remained only one direction: downward. Interest, enthusiasm, investments, and efforts in AI development plummeted, going from hero to zero in less than two decades. However, as we will argue in the next chapter, it would be a mistake to dismiss the rule-based approach entirely. It can still offer elegant and practical solutions to specific problems in many business contexts. The key lies in understanding its strengths and limitations and applying it judiciously where appropriate. This period of disillusionment, known as the "AI winter," lasted from the mid-1970s to the early 1990s. Funding dried up, research slowed, and AI's reputation suffered. However, beneath the surface, an alternative approach to AI was beginning to take root. Instead of attempting to programme every rule explicitly, researchers started to explore the possibility of enabling machines to learn from data. This shift in perspective, propelled by advancements in computer science and the increasing availability of digital data, would eventually lead to AI's resurgence and machine learning's emergence as a dominant paradigm. This new approach addressed some of the limitations of rule-based systems. Rather than necessitating programmers to articulate every rule, machine learning algorithms could discern patterns and relationships from data, allowing them to tackle more complex and nuanced tasks. For instance, rather than defining the rules for recognising a cat in an image, researchers could train a machine-learning model on thousands of pictures of cats and non-cats, enabling the model to learn the distinguishing features of a cat autonomously.

This shift from explicit programming to data-driven learning marked a turning point in the history of AI. It paved the way for developing powerful new techniques, such as deep learning, which have revolutionised fields like computer vision, natural language processing, and robotics. While rule-based systems still have their place, machine learning has emerged as the driving force behind many of the AI applications we see today, from self-driving cars to personalised recommendations. This is not to say that machine learning is a silver bullet. It also has its own set of challenges and limitations. For one, machine learning models are only as good as the data on which they are trained. Biased or incomplete data can lead to inaccurate or unfair predictions. Moreover, the inner workings of these models can be opaque, making it difficult to understand why they make certain decisions—an issue known as the "black box" problem. Despite these challenges, the rise of machine learning has propelled AI out of its winter and into a period of unprecedented growth and innovation. This resurgence has been fuelled by the convergence of several factors, including the exponential growth of data, the availability of powerful and affordable computing resources, and the development of new algorithms and techniques. This "perfect storm" has led to breakthroughs in areas such as image recognition, speech synthesis, and natural language processing, paving the way for the development of applications that were once the stuff of science fiction.

THE NEW HOPE

In class, Mark asks his students when their first contact with AI is. Their responses are often coloured by science fiction and portrayals of AI in popular culture. Terms like "Skynet," "The Matrix," and "singularity" frequently emerge, revealing a deep-seated association of AI with dystopian futures and existential threats. This disconnect between the technical realities of AI and its public perception is a recurring theme in Mark's pedagogy. He uses these preconceived notions, often rooted in fear and misunderstanding, as a springboard for critical discussion. By dissecting the narratives that shape our understanding of AI, Mark encourages his students to engage with this technology's ethical and societal implications, fostering a more nuanced and informed perspective on its potential benefits and risks. When Terence asks in his AI classes when the term "AI" began appearing frequently on students' radars, the most common responses cluster around the 2010s. This perception aligns with the timeline of AI's resurgence, as a new approach to building AI systems began to take root at the turn of the millennium, maturing into practical applications over the following decade. This latest iteration of AI represented a radical departure from earlier attempts, predicated on a probabilistic/statistical rather than deterministic approach. To illustrate this shift, consider the task of identifying a doughnut. Instead of programming a set of rules stating that a doughnut is typically round with a hole in the centre (which raises philosophical questions about the nature of a "hole" or "round"), the new approach involves feeding the algorithm a large number of images and allowing it to discern patterns and probabilities that indicate whether it's looking at a doughnut. The system then receives feedback on the accuracy of its guesses, refining its understanding over time.

This way of doing things effectively flips the previous procedure on its head. Rather than choosing upfront a model and feeding data into it to make it more intelligent, the data itself informs how the task can be performed and how the model should work. This paradigm shift marks the birth of what we now commonly refer to as machine learning. To better understand this mechanism, say you are teaching a friend to recognise music genres. Your (uncultured) friend is utterly unfamiliar with different music styles. You are going to educate him by playing various songs and showing him which genre each belongs to—rock, pop, hip-hop, and so on. Over time, your friend begins to notice specific patterns: rock songs often feature loud guitars, classical music is mainly orchestra-based, while pop songs frequently have catchy choruses. To ensure your friend can get the answers right, whenever he has made a guess, you will confirm or disconfirm whether the guess is correct. Initially, your friend might make numerous mistakes in classification—assigning a song to a genre. However, as you provide more examples, his ability to guess the correct genre improves based on the patterns they've observed. In machine learning, the algorithm assumes the role of your friend. It receives a large volume of data (songs) and labels indicating what each piece of data represents (the genre). After the algorithm guesses the answer, it will check against the label to see whether it got it right, which is no different from when you tell your friend if he has come up with the correct genre. The system learns to identify patterns through this process and eventually makes accurate predictions about new, unlabelled data without explicit instruction. Like your friend becoming more adept at recognising music genres with repeated exercise, the machine learning algorithm becomes increasingly proficient as it encounters more examples. It's important to note that in this scenario, you have a clear outcome in mind—correctly identifying the genre of a given song. This approach is called *supervised learning* in AI speak, where the desired result is known. It's a statistics method used for predicting—or, more accurately, guessing with increasing confidence—an outcome based on a set of input variables, referred to as features.

Supervised learning can produce two types of outputs. The first is the classification of binary categorical outcomes, such as yes/no, high/low, 0/1, or "a cat/not a cat." Alternatively, a supervised learning model can estimate specific numerical outcomes. For instance, a bank can use it to predict the credit card debt of a 28-year-old male with only secondary school education based on available data. In contrast, *unsupervised learning* operates without predefined outcome variables to predict. In other words, you don't know precisely what you're looking for at the outset. By slicing and dicing a large set of data, the algorithm identifies potential outcomes that may or may not be relevant. It will then pass on to human experts to interpret the results and determine their significance and utility.

To illustrate unsupervised learning, imagine being presented with a large basket of fruits, but you've never seen them before and don't know their names. Your task is to sort them into groups based on their characteristics. Examining the fruits, you notice their colours, shapes, sizes, and textures. Without prior knowledge or labels, you begin grouping similar items: perhaps round, red objects with stems in one group; yellow, curved objects with thick peels in another; and small, round purple objects in clusters in a third. Unsupervised learning follows a similar principle. In this scenario, the algorithm, like you, is given data (fruits) without any predefined categories. It must discover patterns and relationships within the data and cluster them into groups. The fruits represent the raw, unlabelled data; your observation of characteristics is analogous to the algorithm analysing features in the data, and the groups you create correspond to the clusters or patterns the algorithm might identify. Just as you grouped the fruits without knowing their names, unsupervised learning algorithms can uncover hidden structures in data without being explicitly told what to look for (especially when you really don't see what you are looking for). This capability makes unsupervised learning particularly valuable for exploratory data analysis and discovering novel insights that might not be apparent through conventional analysis methods.

These two approaches, supervised and unsupervised learning, are the cornerstones of machine learning, a mainstay of traditional AI. They provide the foundation for more complex and sophisticated AI systems. While GenAI, with its capacity to operate like an intern, has captured the public's imagination, it is crucial to remember that these fundamental techniques continue to power a wide range of applications that impact our daily lives. Traditional machine learning remains an essential tool for businesses and organisations across various industries, from recommendation engines that suggest films to systems that identify and monitor data for predictive maintenance. Supervised and unsupervised learning principles have been extended and evolved into deep learning, which employs artificial neural networks with multiple layers to extract increasingly complex patterns from data. Deep learning has demonstrated remarkable capabilities in computer vision, image recognition, natural language processing, and game playing, often surpassing human-level performance. As we delve deeper into AI, it is vital to maintain this historical perspective.

Understanding the evolution of AI, from its early days of rule-based systems to the rise of machine learning and deep learning, enriches our understanding of the field's capabilities and limitations. While the excitement surrounding GenAI is undoubtedly thrilling, it is essential to remember that AI is not a monolithic entity. It encompasses a broad spectrum of techniques and approaches, each with its own strengths and weaknesses. A dynamic interplay between traditional and cutting-edge techniques characterises the current AI landscape. Grasping this interplay is crucial for businesses and individuals seeking to leverage the power of AI. By embracing the lessons of the past and the possibilities of the future, we can navigate the ever-evolving world of AI and unlock its true potential.

GOING IN-DEPTH INTO DEEP LEARNING

It's worth noting that while supervised and unsupervised learning may sound like technologies that have only recently emerged in the AI era, they are fundamentally data-mining and statistical techniques that have been in use for quite some time. Deep learning represents the breakthrough that has led us to today's AI technologies. Despite the power of the methods mentioned above, real-life situations often present complexities far beyond simply identifying a picture of a doughnut or estimating an account balance. For instance, consider the challenge of developing an algorithm capable of writing as skilfully as humans. This task would necessitate gathering and reviewing an extensive amount of information, followed by a lengthy and iterative examination of how proper sentences are constructed. Indeed, this process mirrors how we think "deeply." We repeatedly process information across multiple brain cells until we can make decisions. We don't need to think hard to choose between a latte or cappuccino (we certainly hope!). However, it would be unwise not to think thoroughly when planning your company's strategy. Deep learning emulates this process, creating artificial neural networks that sift through information across multiple layers, each building upon the insights of its predecessors.

To better understand deep learning, think of it as teaching an army of detectives, each with a specific role, to solve a complex mystery by working together. Imagine your team is tasked with solving a crime, but no single detective possesses all the necessary information. The first detective examines initial clues, such as footprints, and passes their findings to the next detective. That detective adds their analysis, perhaps by examining fingerprints, before passing the information on to the next, who might check for DNA evidence. The subsequent detective can look for additional evidence, building on what has previously been uncovered. Each detective in the chain performs their specialised task and relays the results. By the end, the final detective has compiled all the information to solve the crime. In deep learning, each "detective" represents a layer in a neural network. The first layer examines raw data (like pixels in an image), the next layer processes that information further (perhaps recognising edges or shapes), and each subsequent layer continues to build upon the work of its predecessors until the final layer makes a decision, such as identifying a face or predicting a number.

But how do these digital detectives learn and improve over time? In the real world, detective work often improves with accumulated experience.

In our analogy, the last detective in the line, knowing how the crime was ultimately solved, can pass this learning back to the previous detective, who will then reflect and pass the knowledge to their predecessor, and so on ("there is no sign of struggle, so the victim must know the murderer"). Along the way, each detective evaluates their performance and strives to improve in future cases. In machine learning, this process is known as back-propagation. The algorithm moves backwards, starting from the last layer. Each "detective" or node is reprogrammed to adjust the weight it assigns to each of the choices it faces, thereby producing better results over time. Let's consider another example: an everyday scenario, such as leaving work to go home. You have three possible routes: taking metro line 1 followed by line 3, using metro line 2 and then walking, or taking a suburban train and then walking a longer distance. The quickest way home depends on various factors: transport reliability, waiting times between connections, the time you step out of the office, and so forth. By making this journey day after day, you learn from experience (for example, arriving home late or noticing fewer fellow commuters on certain trains) and then consider what caused the longer journey. Over time, you'll likely develop a stronger preference for one specific route based on the conditions of your departure time. Essentially, you've been assigning increasing weight to the option that consistently performs best. This is essentially how machines learn.

Two key developments have enabled machines to operate in this manner. Firstly, the vast amounts of data available on the Internet serve as the raw material for these systems to learn from. Secondly, the advent of graphics processing units (GPUs), made popular—more importantly—cheaper by the rise and rise of the gaming industry, which have later been modified into AI-efficient chips, providing the necessary computational power to process this data efficiently. This technological advancement is one reason companies like Nvidia have become darlings of investors in the GenAI competition. This is also why Intel, which once dominated the computer processor units (CPUs), has missed the AI wave and is performing poorly at the time of writing. In addition to supervised and unsupervised learning, there is another in the machine learning toolkit: reinforcement learning. In this approach, the machine is given "rewards" and "punishments" to indicate whether its actions were correct or not. The algorithm is presented with data that lacks labels but is rewarded when it produces the correct output (such as receiving a point) and punished if the answer is incorrect (such as having the total score deducted).

Imagine a new video game where you must navigate a maze to reach a treasure chest. At the start, you don't know the best way to get there, so you begin exploring. Every time you move, the game provides feedback: if you're going in the right direction, you might hear an upbeat sound or see your score increase; if you're going the wrong way, you might listen to a "got-it-wrong" sound or lose points. Reinforcement learning is, therefore, a type of machine learning where the algorithm (like you in the game) learns how to make decisions by trying different actions and observing the results. Over time, the algorithm determines which actions yield the best rewards (or lead to the treasure chest) and avoids actions that result in poor outcomes.

This ability to learn from feedback and refine its actions over time is what makes reinforcement learning particularly well-suited for tasks that involve decision-making in complex, dynamic environments. For example, reinforcement learning has been utilised to develop AI systems capable of playing games like Go and chess at a superhuman level. These systems learn by playing against themselves millions of times, receiving rewards for winning and punishments for losing. Through this iterative process of trial and error, they gradually develop strategies and tactics that allow them to outperform even the most skilled human players. Reinforcement learning is also finding applications in a growing number of real-world scenarios. For instance, it is being used to optimise traffic flow in cities, control robots in industrial settings, and develop personalised treatment plans for patients with chronic diseases. In each of these cases, the AI system learns by interacting with its environment and receiving feedback on its actions, gradually improving its performance over time.

While reinforcement learning holds immense promise, it also faces certain limitations. One challenge is the need for large amounts of training data. Unlike supervised learning, where the algorithm is given labelled data to learn from, reinforcement learning algorithms must explore their environment and gather their own data through trial and error. This can be a time-consuming and computationally expensive process. Additionally, designing appropriate reward systems for complex tasks can be challenging. If the rewards are not well-defined, the algorithm may learn to exploit loopholes in the system or fail to achieve the desired outcome. Despite these challenges, reinforcement learning remains a vibrant and rapidly developing area of AI research. As our understanding of this powerful technique continues to advance, we can expect to see even more innovative and impactful applications emerge in the years to come. The success of reinforcement learning, like other forms of machine learning, hinges on the availability of high-quality data, efficient algorithms, and powerful computing resources. These factors have converged in recent years to create a fertile environment for AI innovation. As data becomes increasingly abundant, algorithms become more sophisticated, and computing power continues to grow, we can expect to see even more impressive feats of AI in the years to come. However, amidst this excitement, it's crucial to maintain a balanced perspective. AI is not a magic bullet that will solve all our problems. It is a powerful tool that, when wielded responsibly and ethically, has the potential to revolutionise many aspects of our lives. However, like any tool, it can be misused or lead to unintended consequences. As we embrace the possibilities of AI, we must also be mindful of its limitations and potential risks.

BACK TO BASIC

Even though the machine learning techniques have taken a very different approach to AI development, it's crucial not to discount the value of traditional rule-based systems entirely. The "if-then" logic that formed the basis of early AI still has its place in modern applications, particularly in the business context where clear, deterministic rules can be established. Rule-based systems excel when the problem domain is well-defined, and the rules governing decision-making are clear and consistent. For instance, a rule-based system can be highly effective in financial compliance, where regulations dictate specific actions based on well-defined criteria. Similarly, rule-based systems can efficiently flag deviations from established norms in manufacturing quality control, where specific tolerances and parameters must be met.

The strength of rule-based systems lies in their transparency and explainability. Explainability, as the name suggests, refers to our ability to elucidate how a machine reaches its decisions and output. When a decision is made, tracing the logic back to the specific rules that led to that outcome is straightforward. This clarity is precious in industries where decisions need to be audited or explained to regulatory bodies. Deep learning-based models often suffer from the lack of such possibility. In other words, we know how the algorithms are built and work but don't know or understand how they reach a specific decision. Any company that cannot explain to its clients and customers how a decision is reached is putting its reputation at risk. Moreover, rule-based systems can be more efficient and require less computational power for specific tasks than their machine-learning counterparts and certainly GenAI ones. They don't need large datasets for training and can be implemented quickly with well-understood rules, lowering companies' AI building costs. However, it's essential to recognise the limitations of rule-based systems. They struggle with ambiguity and nuance and can't quickly adapt to new situations that weren't explicitly programmed for. This is where machine learning and deep learning shine, with their ability to discern patterns and make decisions in complex, evolving environments.

For example, in a customer service chatbot, initial interactions might be handled by a rule-based system that can efficiently address common queries. Imagine a customer inquiring about store hours or the status of their order—these are straightforward questions with clear-cut answers that can be easily programmed into a rule-based system. The chatbot could be designed to recognise keywords like "hours," "location," or "order status" and instantly provide the relevant information. This ensures a quick and efficient resolution for the customer, especially for simple inquiries. However, when the conversation takes a turn towards more complex issues or nuanced language, the limitations of a rule-based system become apparent. For instance, a customer might describe a problem with a product using subjective terms or ask for recommendations based on their preferences. In such scenarios, a machine-learning model, trained on vast amounts of text data, would be better equipped to understand the customer's intent. This is where the seamless transition comes in. The chatbot could be designed to identify when a query goes beyond its rule-based capabilities, triggering the activation of the machine learning model. This handoff, often imperceptible to the customer, ensures that the chatbot can handle a wider range of interactions, providing a more sophisticated and personalised customer service experience. This hybrid approach represents the power of combining different AI techniques to leverage their respective strengths and compensate for their weaknesses.

As we chart a course ahead for making businesses AI-powered, it's crucial to maintain a balanced perspective. While the allure of cutting-edge technologies like GenAI is undeniable, there's immense value in understanding and leveraging the full spectrum of AI approaches, from classical rule-based systems to the latest developments in agentic AI. By appreciating the strengths and limitations of each approach, businesses can make informed decisions about which technologies to apply to specific challenges. This is what we will turn to.

CHAPTER 3

Traditional AI in Current Business Use

THE USE OF AI in business has been well-documented over the past decade. Several books and consulting reports have examined the direction of industry sectors in terms of AI adoption, while others have focused on the AI strategies of large companies. This chapter, however, takes a different approach. Rather than providing a broad overview or speculating on future trends, we aim to offer a practical guide that will equip organisations with the necessary knowledge and tools to confidently and effectively leverage AI for transformative growth, reassuring them that they are on the right path. We aim to provide insights into the essential steps and best practices for initiating and executing AI projects. By distilling lessons learned from our engagements with clients across various sectors, we aim to equip readers with the knowledge and tools necessary to embark on their AI journey with confidence and effectiveness. They are designed to be indispensable ideas for organisations of all sizes, from startups to established enterprises, ensuring that everyone can harness the power of AI to drive innovation and efficiency in their operations.

To achieve this goal, we have structured the chapter into several key sections, each addressing a crucial aspect of AI implementation. We begin by highlighting some success factors that all companies should be aware of. Next, we delve into the process of identifying suitable AI use cases within an organisation. One recurring theme that becomes apparent is that AI solutions don't rely solely on the models—they cannot exist in a

DOI: 10.1201/9781003559665-3

vacuum. A practical solution requires all the components surrounding the models to work well and collaboratively. This will be featured repeatedly in our description of AI use cases and how our core platform at Nexus FrontierTech operates. Subsequently, we will offer eight recommendations for implementing AI in business.

TRADITIONAL AI = BESPOKE AI SOLUTIONS

The versatility of AI technology is both its greatest strength and a potential source of confusion for businesses considering its adoption. Each organisation has unique challenges, processes, and goals, necessitating a tailored approach to AI implementation. What works for a large e-commerce company may not be suitable for a small manufacturing firm, and vice versa. When discussing AI in a business context, it is crucial to understand that there is no one-size-fits-all solution. AI is a highly adaptable tool, and while there are numerous ways to deploy it in today's business landscape, our experience with clients over the years has demonstrated that off-the-shelf AI technologies rarely meet the precise needs of a specific business. However, it is essential to recognise that the inability to find a perfect off-the-shelf AI solution differs significantly from the ability to utilise off-the-shelf AI/ML models. The use of pre-trained models has become increasingly prevalent in recent years, with many companies embracing this trend by utilising and fine-tuning existing AI models for their specific use cases rather than building everything from scratch.

This trend in the AI landscape has led to a proliferation of ready-to-use models that can be selected from and seamlessly integrated into existing AI systems. The flexibility and accessibility of these models have undoubtedly accelerated the adoption of AI across various industries. However, the availability of these models does not diminish the need for careful consideration and customisation in AI implementation. While pre-trained models provide a strong foundation, they still require substantial work to integrate effectively into a company's broader systems and processes. Moreover, companies must thoroughly evaluate the suitability of pre-trained models for their specific use cases. Factors such as the model's training data, potential biases, and limitations must be thoroughly understood to ensure ethical and effective deployment. In some instances, a combination of pre-trained models and custom-developed components may be required to achieve the desired functionality. The trend towards using pre-trained models also highlights the importance of keeping abreast of the rapidly evolving AI landscape. As new models are developed and released, companies need to regularly assess whether their current AI systems could benefit from upgrades or replacements. This necessitates ongoing investment in AI literacy and expertise within the organisation, as well as a commitment to continuous improvement and adaptation. This also underscores a crucial point for ensuring AI is a business success: AI models are merely a part of the overall system that companies must consider and integrate comprehensively.

BEYOND MODELS: THE IMPORTANCE OF HOLISTIC INTEGRATION

What truly makes AI deployment in business testing challenging are the other system issues surrounding the AI models, which extend far beyond the technical capabilities of the models themselves. These aspects often make or break an AI initiative. Yet, they are frequently overlooked in the excitement surrounding cutting-edge AI technologies. For instance, many AI vendors have repeatedly ignored the fact that the user interface often determines whether their clients can fully leverage their technologies. After all, how and why would any employee be motivated and inclined to use an AI system if it is clunky, difficult to navigate, and not aesthetically pleasing? The importance of user experience in AI system adoption cannot be overstated. Or, as we examine in the later chapter, are the workers themselves given enough training? Another critical, yet often under-appreciated, aspect of AI deployment is data infrastructure. AI models are only as good as the data they're trained on and have access to. Many organisations find their existing data systems are inadequate for supporting AI applications. Issues such as data silos, inconsistent data formats, poor data quality, and lack of real-time data access can significantly hinder AI performance and reliability. Addressing these data challenges often requires substantial investment in data infrastructure, including data warehouses, data lakes, and robust data governance processes.

A further important factor is the integration of AI systems with existing business processes and legacy systems. Many businesses have complex, long-standing operational systems that are not easily compatible with new AI technologies. Integrating AI into workflows can be time-consuming, costly, and fraught with technical challenges. It often requires careful planning, extensive testing, and sometimes even a complete overhaul of existing systems to ensure smooth integration and optimal performance. Just as vital to the success of any AI adoption is meeting the broader challenge of change management. Introducing AI into an organisation can create anxiety among employees who may fear job displacement or feel ill-equipped to work with new technologies. Terence was once invited by a large bank as a speaker on the subject of AI to its branch staff. He was instructed by the organiser not to mention potential job losses as it would create fear. Overcoming staff resistance requires clear communication, comprehensive training programmes, and sometimes a cultural shift within the organisation to embrace AI as a tool for augmentation rather than replacement. Ethical considerations and regulatory compliance also play a crucial role in the deployment of AI. As AI systems become more prevalent and influential in decision-making processes, concerns about bias, fairness, transparency, and privacy have come to the forefront. Organisations must navigate complex ethical landscapes and ensure their AI systems comply with evolving regulations, such as the General Data Protection Regulation (GDPR) in Europe or the California Consumer Privacy Act (CCPA) in California. This often necessitates the development of robust governance frameworks and ethical guidelines for AI use.

Scalability and maintenance of AI systems present another set of challenges. An AI solution that performs well in a pilot or small-scale deployment may encounter significant challenges when scaled up to enterprise-level operations. Issues such as computational resources, model drift (where the performance of an AI model degrades over time as the real-world data it encounters differs from its training data), and the need for continuous monitoring and updating of AI systems all need to be addressed for long-term success. The cost factor of AI deployment is also a significant consideration. While AI can offer substantial returns on investment, the initial costs of implementation can be high. This includes not just the cost of AI technologies themselves but also the associated costs of data infrastructure upgrades, integration efforts, training, and ongoing maintenance. Organisations need to carefully assess the total cost of ownership and potential return on investment when planning AI initiatives. Lastly, the shortage of AI talent remains a persistent challenge for many organisations. Deploying and maintaining AI systems requires specialised skills that are in high demand and short supply. This talent crunch can slow down AI initiatives and drive up costs. Organisations often need to develop strategies for attracting and retaining AI talent or consider partnerships with external AI experts and service providers.

THE CRITICAL ROLE OF AI OPERATIONS (AIOPS)

As early as 2020, we identified that one of the most common reasons AI projects fail in companies is that they have overlooked the importance of AI Operations (AIOps), or more commonly known as ML Operations (MLOps). The simple fact is that integrating AI models into a company's overall technology architecture is challenging and demanding. AIOps is the practice of building, integrating, testing, releasing, deploying, and managing the system to turn AI model results into desired insights for end-users. It's a critical component that bridges the gap between the potential of AI models and their practical application in a business setting. To better understand the role of AIOps, consider this analogy: an AI model is like a high-performance car engine. While it's an impressive piece of technology on its own, a business is fundamentally seeking not just an exquisite piece of engineering; instead, it needs to get from point A to point B efficiently and reliably.[1] The rest of the vehicle—the transmission, the chassis, the wheels, the steering system—is needed to help make the journey and maximise what the engine can offer.

Just as assembling a car requires not only the components but also the knowledge, experience, and expertise to make these components work together in harmony, implementing AI in a business necessitates a similar approach. This holistic strategy to AI implementation lies at the heart of successful AI projects. The importance of AIOps becomes increasingly apparent when considering the dynamic nature of business environments. AI models, once deployed, are not static entities. They require continuous monitoring, updating, and optimisation to maintain their performance and relevance, keeping pace with market demand. This ongoing management is a crucial aspect of AIOps. For instance, consider a retail company that implements an AI-driven inventory management system. The initial deployment may yield impressive results, but as consumer behaviours change, market trends shift, or new products are introduced, the AI model's predictions may become less accurate over time. AIOps practices ensure that these changes are detected, the model is retrained with new data, and the system continues to provide valuable insights.

Moreover, AIOps plays a critical role in ensuring the reliability and scalability of AI systems. As AI becomes more integral to business operations, any downtime or performance issues can have significant consequences. AIOps encompasses practices such as automated monitoring, anomaly detection, and rapid troubleshooting to maintain system health and minimise disruptions. Furthermore, AIOps contributes significantly to the governance and compliance aspects of AI deployment. As regulations surrounding AI use continue to evolve, organisations need robust systems to track model lineage, monitor for bias, and ensure transparency in AI decision-making. AIOps practices can help establish these governance structures, making it easier for companies to demonstrate responsible AI use to regulators and stakeholders.

THE ETHICS OF AI BEYOND JUST ETHICS

Recognising the importance of ethical considerations in AI adoption is crucial for fostering trust and ensuring that these technologies are used for the greater good. Responsible AI practices are essential for mitigating the potential risks associated with AI systems, such as biases, lack of transparency, and privacy concerns. By dedicating a section to this critical topic, we aim to provide comprehensive guidance on ensuring that AI systems operate fairly, transparently, and accountably. Addressing biases is vital, as AI systems can inadvertently perpetuate existing societal prejudices if not managed with care. This necessitates implementing robust methods for identifying and correcting biases within data and algorithms. Transparency in AI is equally essential, requiring clear communication about how AI systems function, make decisions, and affect stakeholders. This ensures that users and those impacted by AI systems can understand their workings and trust their outcomes.

Accountability in AI necessitates that organisations establish clear governance frameworks and ethical guidelines. These frameworks should clearly delineate the responsibilities of developers, users, and organisations throughout the AI lifecycle, ensuring that ethical principles are consistently maintained. Privacy concerns must also be prioritised, with rigorous measures in place to protect personal data and uphold user confidentiality. In addition to these technical and procedural considerations, cultivating an organisational culture that prioritises ethics in AI is essential. Training and educating stakeholders on potential ethical dilemmas and the significance of responsible AI behaviour can further enhance the adoption of these practices. Collaboration among industry leaders, policymakers, and academics is equally vital for creating standards and sharing best practices across various sectors. Ultimately, responsible AI practices safeguard against ethical pitfalls, ensuring that AI advancements benefit society as a whole while respecting individual rights and promoting fairness, equality, and social justice.

THE HUMAN ELEMENT IN AI IMPLEMENTATION

The weak points in AI implementation are not always technological or even technical. A company's culture, management team, employees, and the ability to engage in change management can all impede and hinder what even the best AI models can achieve. Factors such as resistance to change, lack of understanding of AI's potential, and insufficient communication can create significant barriers. In short, successful AI implementation is often not just an engineering problem but a social one. Engineering solutions alone cannot solve social problems. This realisation underscores the need for a multidisciplinary approach to AI adoption, considering technological, operational, and human factors in equal measure. The human aspect involves fostering a culture of innovation, ensuring employee buy-in, and equipping staff with the necessary skills and knowledge to work alongside AI technologies.

HOW AN AI SYSTEM WORKS

The ideas and insights we present in this chapter (and in Chapter 4) are not merely theoretical; they are grounded in real-world applications and the latest advancements in AI technology. We draw upon extensive research, industry case studies, and collaboration with AI experts, ensuring that our insights remain practical and applicable. While countless methods exist for implementing AI in business, each company's journey is unique, shaped by its specific challenges and opportunities. By sharing our approach, we aim to inspire businesses to discover their path to AI success. We explore various strategies and frameworks that have proven effective across different industries, supplying concrete examples of how AI can drive innovation, streamline operations, and enhance decision-making. Additionally, we discuss successful transformations and lessons learned from failures, providing a balanced view of AI integration. Our goal is to empower businesses to confidently embark on their AI journey, fostering a culture of continuous learning and adaptation to remain ahead in an ever-evolving technological landscape. Ultimately, we seek to spark creativity and ambition, encouraging leaders to harness AI's potential to transform their organisations and achieve sustainable growth.

Let's get back down to business. At this juncture in AI technology development and evolution, traditional AI is best suited for assisting companies with their behind-the-scenes activities, including back- and middle-office operations. These are probably why, according to a recent study on how

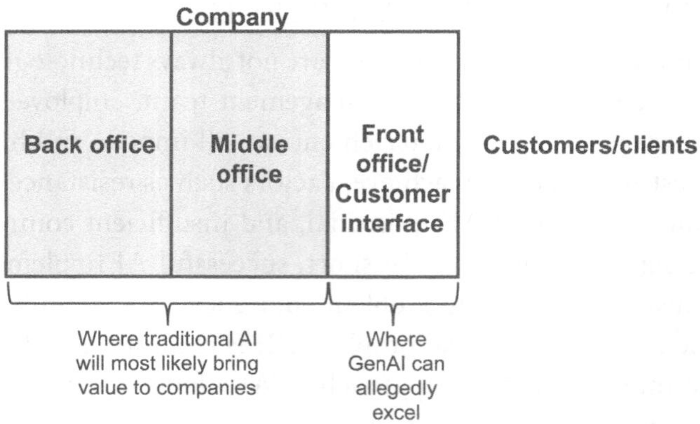

FIGURE 3.1 Where traditional and generative AI can excel.

companies are adopting AI, employee productivity and cost management account for almost half of the responses when the respondents were asked which is the most critical business outcome they are trying to achieve.[2] Not surprisingly, the same report also found that 43% of the use cases are related to individual employee productivity and efficiency, such as reducing time spent analysing or completing tasks.

These ideas are shown in **Figure 3.1**.

It's important to note that this is not a strict rule—traditional AI can be used to interact with customers or clients, just as generative AI (GenAI) can also be used for internal communication. As we'll discuss in Chapter 4, we have integrated GenAI into backend automation in our client work. However, for the moment, let's focus on traditional AI.

WHY SHOULD COMPANIES START WITH TRADITIONAL AI?

From a technology perspective, it makes sense for companies to start with traditional AI because it has been repeatedly tested and refined over many years. The technology represents a tried-and-true approach that leverages established algorithms and methodologies honed through extensive use, providing a robust framework upon which businesses can rely. It has matured enough to lower the risk of implementation failure, making it a safer bet for companies new to AI adoption. By starting with well-understood models, companies can find it easier to familiarise themselves with—and hence create value from—AI's capabilities and limitations. Given that traditional AI is costly and must be custom-built, it forces businesses to identify and work out in detail the best and most valuable automation opportunities. From a business perspective, starting with AI in the middle and back office gives companies far more control over managing problems during development. In addition, this strategic focus can often open up opportunities for organisations to optimise internal processes, enhance operational efficiency, and establish a foundation of trust in AI technologies. Moreover, by resolving behind-the-scenes challenges, companies can fine-tune algorithms and adjust parameters without the pressure of direct customer interaction, thus safeguarding their brand reputation.

Brand (and hence customer trust) is particularly crucial for our financial services clients, who cannot afford to make mistakes when their customers' money is involved. The stakes are too high for experimentation in customer-facing applications without a solid foundation of AI experience and expertise. In the finance sector, where precision and reliability are paramount, missteps can lead to severe consequences, including financial loss and erosion of trust. Therefore, away from the prying eye of customers and clients, companies have the time to build up experience, expertise and confidence in their systems, ensuring they are fully prepared for any eventual expansion into customer-facing roles. Such a cautious approach mitigates risk, reinforces customer trust, and lays the groundwork for effective long-term AI deployment.

ILLUSTRATION #1: AI SOLUTIONS

Let's now turn to examine how companies have adopted and can continue to adopt AI solutions. These are drawn directly from client experience. Admittedly, they are all related to financial services. However, they showcase how traditional AI can help companies create value. The fundamentals of these solutions, we believe, are equally applicable to businesses in many other sectors.

Opening a New Market

Traditionally, commercial loans of less than £10 million to small and medium-sized enterprises (SMEs) have represented an unprofitable and, therefore, neglected market. The lack of economic opportunities arises from the fact that banks must deploy teams of relationship managers and credit and risk analysts, spending considerable time manually conducting "financial spreading" (a process used to extract financial data and line items from balance sheets, income statements, and cash flow statements, which are then entered and organised into databases and systems). As a result, global banks focus their resources on offering loans to listed and large private companies, thereby overlooking opportunities to lend to SMEs. AI has altered the landscape by utilising machines to perform financial spreading swiftly and, crucially, accurately. The reliable financial data disclosures are subsequently converted into various output formats and reports, along with standardised risk indicators for credit assessment. By reducing these costs, banks can profitably access this previously unprofitable market volume.

Enhancing Processing Activities

By automating its mortgage approval process, we enabled a global UK-based bank to generate £10 million in annual savings. Previously, this approval procedure involved 22 checkpoints, with the initial one requiring human workers to scrutinise applicants' submitted data and enter it into the system. Following this, the sales quality team reviews the applications to ensure compliance with regulations. It comprises a total of 120 reviewers who must sift through ten data sources to extract the necessary information from 180 data points for audits. Each compliance review takes approximately four hours. The bank has automated data extraction using AI technologies, reducing compliance processing time by over 80%. This solution has dramatically enhanced operational efficiency and effectiveness, minimising human errors, mitigating compliance risks, and optimising the overall processes.

Increasing Reporting Reliability

Few people enjoy writing reports, and even fewer take pleasure in summarising activities and producing daily reports at the end of each workday. Meanwhile, companies seek to minimise the costs linked to their staff dedicating time to such reporting activities. Nevertheless, these reports are essential for the management and governance of the company. An international UK asset manager requires its accounting teams to maintain precise daily records of fund performance and transactions to calculate the value of each fund portfolio and ensure compliance with regulatory reporting requirements. However, manually processing data from various financial documents is both time-consuming and susceptible to errors. Traditional optical character recognition (OCR) techniques struggle to handle complex documents, often necessitating extensive manual verification, which can lead to delays in fund valuation and reporting. We developed a highly accurate AI data parsing solution for this asset manager.

The system achieves 97% accuracy in extracting and categorising financial data from diverse documents, employing models specifically trained on financial materials. The outcome: our client can dramatically reduce manual processing time while producing exceptionally accurate reports promptly.

Using a RegBot to Help Complete Forms

A forward-looking global market regulator in the Middle East aiming to elevate its financial centre status has offered to assist companies applying for membership in achieving better compliance and risk management outcomes, as well as reducing application burdens. We developed a "RegBot" powered by natural language processing (NLP) and machine learning to streamline the application process. The robot can automatically complete forms and perform gap analyses to identify and clarify any missing or inconsistent data, all in real time. Once the form is accurately filled in, the robot generates comprehensive assessment reports for the regulator, making it easier and quicker to review applications and make decisions.

Improving Personal Account Dealing

Investment firms must consistently manage regulatory compliance, conflict management, trade monitoring, and reporting for personal account dealing (PAD). However, this is easier said than done. High trade volumes and the complexity of the business often result in insufficient staff verification, allowing executed trades to go unchecked. It is not uncommon for only a tiny fraction of trades to be verified despite an increase in personnel numbers. Regulatory compliance issues will continue to accumulate. AI can efficiently track every trading transaction and extract all necessary data points, entering them in the correct fields on the PAD management platform, which must be supported by extensive end-user training. This system can automatically perform compliance checks, monitor conflicts, and oversee trade processes, ensuring the capturing of all transactions and accurate reporting by the end of the day.

Assisting Compliance Checkers

In the UK, companies that sell fund products to retail customers are legally obliged to restrict their communications to a narrow range of themes and subjects, using predetermined scripts. This is intended to prevent misselling. The compliance teams at these firms, as well as similar ones, often must manually review transcribed calls and emails to ensure that sales brokers adhere to scripts and comply with investment regulations. These checks require examining a vast amount of communication data with great scrutiny. Inevitably, errors occur during these time-consuming activities. However, these companies have no choice but to continue investing resources into this cost centre merely to maintain regulatory compliance. An AI-powered solution can swiftly analyse call recordings and emails, providing real-time compliance checks against predefined scripts and regulatory requirements. This leads to a significant reduction in the workload of human checkers, allowing them to concentrate on managing borderline and exceptional cases, as well as supervising the AI. With increased process efficiency and reduced human error, this not only improves quality but also provides a cost-effective and scalable solution for firms to monitor customer communications.

Tracking Down Companies' Extensive Subsidiaries

Banks today are navigating an increasingly complex and challenging regulatory environment, where traditional compliance methods struggle to keep pace. At the heart of modern risk management lies a deceptively simple question: Who exactly are you doing business with? Banks need to know the precise answer to avoid being used for money laundering. An AI-powered legal entity identifier (LEI) is essentially a digital fingerprint for legal entities—a globally recognised 20-character alphanumeric code that uniquely identifies companies engaged in financial transactions. For instance, if a bank is onboarding a client with indirect ties to a sanctioned company through multiple offshore entities—a single multinational might operate under dozens of names across different jurisdictions—AI-driven LEI systems can uncover this hidden relationship before a single pound is moved. Algorithms can rapidly sift through vast amounts of unstructured data, such as corporate filings, public registries, and transaction records, matching these data points to the correct entities. The technology also scans text-based data, such as legal disclosures or media reports, to identify potential red flags that may not be apparent through traditional compliance checks. This process, which is performed automatically, swiftly, and inexpensively, is known as entity resolution. When performed manually, it is notoriously complex and costly, if possible at all. Banks that implement AI-enhanced LEIs experience faster onboarding, sharper fraud detection, fewer compliance lapses, and significantly less time and money spent on remediation.

ILLUSTRATION #2: THE ONENEXUS PLATFORM

Having looked at the various use cases, let's double-click them to look at how an AI system works in practice. The "OneNexus" platform shown in **Figure 3.2** is our modular, scalable AI solution that we have been offering to our financial services clients to streamline document processing workflows substantially. This platform is the culmination of years of technical and business experience, as well as best practices and innovative thinking. Again, while the underlying principles are most relevant to financial services, they are applicable across various industries.

The first immediate observation is that for AI to work effectively in business, the models and core algorithms are merely one part of a larger platform or system. As mentioned in our discussion on AIOps, the key to realising AI's intended benefits is not solely to focus on the models themselves. Instead, it's about ensuring that every component works together like a well-tuned orchestra. Any part that doesn't function well will prevent the AI system from operating at its full potential. As the O-ring theory dictates, a system is only as strong as its weakest component. This underscores the vital need for a holistic approach to AI implementation, where each element receives equal attention and care. While different AI vendors may have varying approaches, OneNexus operates with four elements that we believe are essential for achieving business success:

Flexible input ingestion: The system accepts—or, using industry terminology, ingests—a diverse range of input formats (point 1 in **Figure 3.2**). In our case, we provide a unified platform to accommodate various documents in different digital formats, essential for a wide range of financial services tasks, including loan approvals, know-your-customer processes, and the latest company news. From a business perspective, the more types and formats of documents a system can ingest, the greater the economies of scale a company can achieve, spreading the investment cost across more aspects of the business.

Layered technology structure: The system is fundamentally supported by three technology layers (point 2 in **Figure 3.2**):

a. At the bottom is the infrastructure layer, which companies must consider in a flexible, secure, and regulatory-compliant manner (e.g., data-sensitive industries such as financial services have stringent and particular regulations) to deploy and establish a centralised, cost-effective platform that can automate various tasks.
b. The data layer lies in the middle. The key is not merely to securely store source documents and verified data with metadata. What's just as

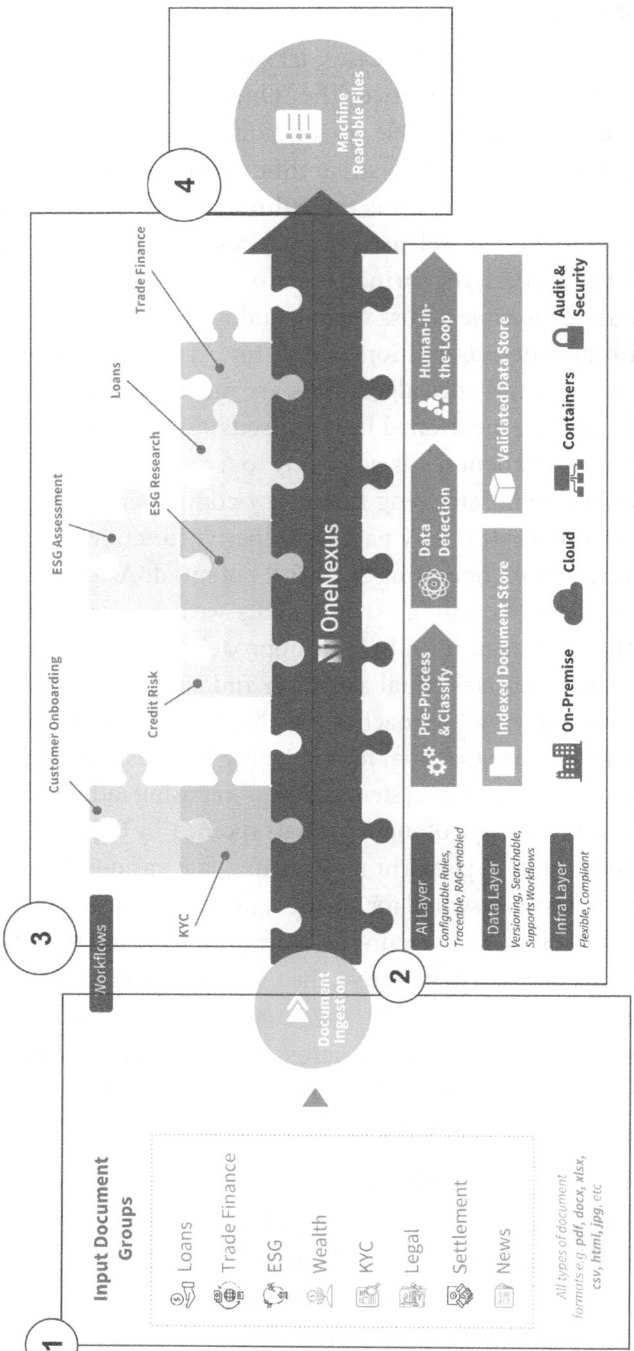

FIGURE 3.2 The "OneNexus" platform.

important is that the layer must provide efficient historical search, possess version control, and reliably maintain linkages to the company's workflows.

c. At the top is the AI layer, where trained AI models accurately recognise and extract data, utilising computer vision, NLP, and GenAI techniques, drawing on the data stored in the infrastructure.

Efficient workflow organisation: Properly organising the workflows (point 3 in **Figure 3.2**) is where business AI makes or breaks. We believe this is where OneNexus excels as a technology platform. Two critical factors are at play here and will be repeated throughout the book: data traceability and human-in-the-loop processes. The ability to trace AI-obtained output to a source is vital. Companies must ensure that data lineage is prominent in their technology stacks, processes, and workflows. Only in this way can companies be fully aware that they are using the correct source data. Often, only humans can discern whether a source is credible. This underscores the second critical factor: embracing the "human-in-the-loop" or "expert-in-the-loop" approach is vital for constructing an infallible AI system. Regardless of how powerful AI technologies may seem, their capabilities are constrained by the extent to which humans engage in guiding and validating their outputs. The "jigsaw" pieces shown in the figure represent the AI models for various functions that AI can perform, such as automated customer onboarding and credit risk assessment. With a platform like OneNexus, our clients can swiftly, efficiently, and affordably expand the use of AI to achieve various business outcomes without needing to start afresh each time. This translates into an effective scaling solution. Moreover, companies can use the platform as a conduit to apply the models in a synchronised manner, creating additional operational benefits.

Usable and integrated output: As output, the AI-powered workflows should produce structured and validated data via APIs or be exported in various digital file formats, such as CSV, JSON, XML, XLS, and PDF. This ensures not just the usability of the output but also helps to further the case for economies of scale. Alternatively, the output should be shown on a well-designed user interface. Many technology vendors have great models and methodologies. Yet, a good number of them appear to have forgotten that even the best AI is useless if the end users are unable—or even worse, unwilling—to interact with and leverage its insights. This is why OneNexus offers a customisable, user-friendly interface that can be personalised to suit the different needs of our clients. **Figure 3.3** shows an example of our user interface.

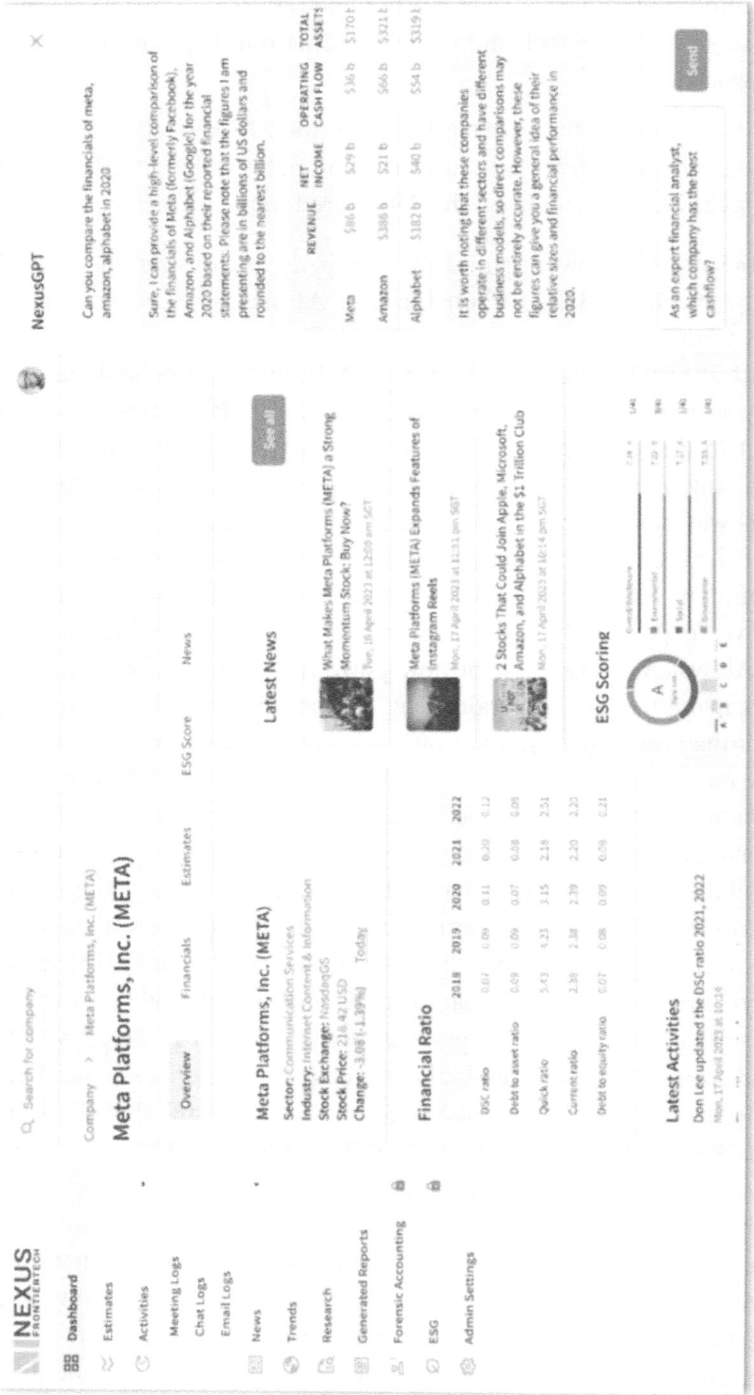

FIGURE 3.3 A user interface created by Nexus FrontierTech.

These four key elements of the OneNexus platform display that a successful AI system in business must look far beyond just implementing advanced algorithms. It requires careful consideration of data input, technology infrastructure, workflow organisation, and output usability. This holistic approach can very often be what sets successful AI implementations apart from those that fail to deliver on their promises.

WHAT TO BEAR IN MIND WHEN THINKING ABOUT AI

As AI technologies evolve and mature, so must our approach to their implementation in business settings. Our previous book outlined five key action points to consider when evaluating the use of AI in business. While some of these points remain relevant, others have diminished in importance as the AI landscape has evolved. Let's revisit these points and introduce three new considerations that reflect the current state of AI in business.

1. Be narrow-minded: This remains a crucial point. Don't try to boil the ocean by becoming an AI-powered company overnight. Instead, identify a task that can be best automated and start there. This focused approach allows for quicker wins and valuable learning experiences.
2. Weigh the risk: This consideration has become less significant in today's business landscape. As traditional AI technologies have developed and proven their reliability, the perceived risk of entrusting AI to make certain decisions has diminished. Nevertheless, it's still crucial to carefully evaluate the potential impacts of AI-driven decisions. Arguably, this concern is increasingly relevant to GenAI, as its adoption in business remains quite uneven (more on this in a later chapter).
3. Get the "last mile" right: This point is more important than ever. There are many activities where machines can perform much better than humans. However, the opposite is also true. Therefore, being able to assign tasks to the party that can best handle them is essential, such as using machines for common cases. In contrast, humans tackle the exceptional and unique ones.
4. Consider that less is more: This is becoming less of an issue in today's business operations. Companies and managers were once obsessed with collating vast amounts of data or having "big data," believing

this was the only way to leverage AI. The truth is, both then and now, the amount of data required depends on the task to be automated. In our experience, using an algorithm to "read" and extract data from driver licenses with an accuracy of 95% requires only about 100 data points. This is a far cry from the big data that is generally considered necessary.

5. Do the necessary homework: This is less of a problem nowadays. Unlike several years ago, many managers are now much more familiar with and knowledgeable about AI. The result is that when planning how to use it, the ideas are no longer as abstract as they once were. They now spend more time thinking through what could and would not work. In fact, with organisations becoming increasingly complex, doing proper homework certainly helps when considering AI.

   As the nature of AI evolves and continues to improve, its application has changed. At the same time, our instinct, ability, and understanding of these technologies have also progressed. Inevitably, new considerations have emerged. We want to add three new action points to our list:

6. Follow the money: To evaluate the financial investments in AI, companies must estimate their return on investment (ROI). This can be significantly more challenging than it appears, as future returns are fraught with uncertainties. It's no surprise that most AI business applications focus on cost savings—achieving outcomes with greater certainty is far more manageable. ROI exists in two forms: hard and soft. "Hard ROI" refers to measurable outcomes such as time saved and productivity increases. In contrast, "soft ROI" involves enhancements to employee experience and the capability to adapt to new opportunities, which are not easily quantified. This illustrates that evaluating the return on investment (ROI) of AI is a complex and nuanced task. Therefore, business managers must identify potential projects that offer the highest return on investment (ROI) and consider practical ways to measure it.

7. Think big, think scale-up: Sometimes, the easiest projects offer short-term gains but may not be the most beneficial in the long run. Choosing an "easy-to-do" project is also tempting. Starting small is indeed a great idea. However, this doesn't mean that companies cannot consider how to scale up if the small project becomes a runaway

success. The challenge here is that the pathways and fundamentals for scaling up may need to be addressed at the outset of the AI project. Companies also need to recognise how complex it is to embrace AI. The methods used to solve problems along the way may create future challenges for scaling up. Managers must continually consider the requirements for the larger-scale adoption of AI.

8. Consider going Z–A instead of just A–Z: When starting an AI project, we often focus on the AI model and how to train it. Yet, this can frequently be the wrong approach—what is far more critical is whether the AI output can be efficiently utilised. This goes beyond merely building an excellent user interface; companies must carefully consider what the AI should produce and the value propositions its output can offer. For instance, if you are creating an AI to automate the processing of loan applications, instead of asking which AI models would help you achieve your goals, you are much better off starting with the specific outcomes that need to be created to deliver value. Do you want the system to recommend the correct interest rate to charge a potential customer, or do you want bank staff to have a full view of all the applicant's details so they can engage with the applicant knowledgeably? Only by doing this can the AI built align with a value proposition—the value proposition that best meets your needs. This also underscores an essential point about AI: Business AI is much more about business than it is about AI.

In this chapter, we examine the various aspects of making AI systems work and embedding them into business operations. Indeed, it is now less of a technological challenge to deploy algorithms for creating business value as the technology matures. Instead, it has primarily become a business challenge, presenting managers and executives with numerous difficulties. As if that were not enough, 30 November 2022, marks the day when AI for business transitions to the next phase, further complicating the lives of managers and executives. It was the day OpenAI's ChatGPT was released to the public. The arrival of GenAI introduces both new opportunities and challenges for companies. While traditional AI continues to play a crucial role in business operations, particularly in back-office and middle-office functions, the emergence of GenAI has expanded the possibilities for customer-facing applications and creative tasks. As we move forward, businesses must be prepared to integrate both traditional AI and GenAI into their operations, leveraging the strengths of each to drive innovation and efficiency. In the following two chapters, we will delve deeper into how GenAI works and what it can and cannot do for businesses, providing a comprehensive understanding of the current AI landscape and its implications for your organisation.

NOTES

1 Tse, Terence, Esposito, Mark, Mizuno, Takaaki Mizuno and Goh, Danny (2020) "The dumb reason your AI project will fail," *Harvard Business Review*, June 8, https://hbr.org/2020/06/the-dumb-reason-your-ai-project-will-fail. Accessed on 26 March 2025.

2 Jyoti, Ritu and Schubmehl, Dave (2024) "2024 Business Opportunity of AI: Generative AI delivering new business value and increasing ROI," *IDC*, https://blogs.microsoft.com/blog/2024/11/12/idcs-2024-ai-opportunity-study-top-five-ai-trends-to-watch/. Accessed on 16 November 2024.

CHAPTER 4

What Is GenAI?

What Are Its Current Limitations?

WHO SAYS SCIENCE FICTION is only for entertainment and has no value in real life? The 2016 film *Arrival* was about a linguist who discovers how to communicate with extraterrestrials who have arrived on Earth. The film was based on the novella, *Story of Your Life,* by the renowned science fiction writer Ted Chiang. Avoiding any spoilers, the alien language of these did not contain linear sequences of words. Instead, they generated entire sentences using a single symbol that represented an idea or a concept, which the human linguist has to work out how to read as a whole. An AI researcher, Illia Polosukhin, believed that the idea of "self-attention"—a central concept to generative AI (GenAI) (as discussed below)—is akin to an extraterrestrial language, which could potentially significantly speed up and augment how machines understand language.[1] The idea was thoroughly explored and published as "Attention is All You Need," a landmark 2017 machine learning research paper authored by eight Google scientists that introduced a new deep-learning architecture known as the Transformer.[2]

This has effectively established the starting point of GenAI as we know it. It represents a groundbreaking class of AI techniques and models specifically engineered to generate new output that closely resembles, but is not directly copied from, the data on which it has been trained. In contrast to traditional AI, which primarily focuses on recognising patterns within existing datasets to make predictions

DOI: 10.1201/9781003559665-4

or classifications, GenAI delves deeper into understanding the fundamental structure of the data itself, developing the capability to create something new. This novelty has opened up previously unseen possibilities—and potentially many value-creating opportunities—for businesses. This chapter aims to comprehensively explore GenAI technology and describe its defining features in detail, illuminating the transformative implications of this groundbreaking development in the AI space. By double-clicking the inner workings of GenAI, we unveil the intricate algorithms and techniques that underpin its remarkable capabilities, providing readers with a nuanced understanding of its potential applications and limitations.

HOW TRANSFORMERS TRANSFORM THE WAY MACHINES DEAL WITH WORDS

Let's start with what many of us can see and use but often don't know what its name even stands for: the GPT in ChatGPT. The "G" refers to generative—as in GenAI. GenAI is software that can produce plausible and sophisticated text, images and computer code at a level that mimics human ability. It is "generative" because of its ability to "create" something new. "P," on the other hand, stands for "pre-trained." Unlike the traditional AI discussed in the previous chapters, users can directly tap into the power of GenAI applications and make immediate use of AI, such as ChatGPT, without introducing data to train any models under the bonnet. As can be imagined, the "T" refers to the transformer concept briefly described above. But how does this work in practice? Here, we can use a simple sentence to provide an overview of the thinking underneath GenAI.

I run a small company that sells technology.

This queried sentence is split into chunks of characters called tokens. These tokens can be words like "small" or "company," affixes such as "pre" or "ised," and punctuation including "?." (This is why many would say one token is *almost* counted as one word on GenAI). So, we can see that our sentence will be separated into individual tokens.

I	run	a	small	company	that	sells	technology

We will attempt to get the machine to "understand" each token. However, it may be difficult for machines to grasp the meaning of the word “run,” given that it can have at least 15 different meanings depending on the context, including:

1. Movement
2. Operation
3. Flow
4. Duration
5. Manage
6. Function
7. Competition
8. Escape
9. Sequence
10. Streak
11. Publish
12. Cost
13. Risk
14. Melt
15. Tear

The trick to getting computers to comprehend different meanings of a word is for them to remember the nearby words using an enormous amount of data (and with this, you should be able to see why large language models (LLMs), such as ChatGPT, are called as such). In the following example, machines take note of only the two neighbouring words on each side of the token “run.”

			I	run	every	morning	to	stay	fit
			I	run	a	small	company	that	sells
		The	river	runs	through	the	valley		
		The	road	runs	along	the	coast		
			He	runs	the	marketing	functions		
		The	car	runs	smoothly				
			She	runs	in	the	local	marathon	every
			He	ran	from	the	crime	scene	
		The	play	runs	for	three	hours		
is	On	the	winning	run					

(Continued)

The newspaper	runs	a	weekly	column	on	technology	
The project	runs	into	millions	of	dollars		
You	run	the	risk	of	getting	caught	
The paint	runs	when	it	gets	too	hot	
Her eyes	ran	with	tears				

However, this only shows what is next to a token and not how they relate to each other. The next step, word embedding, is where things get interesting. Imagine you have a big box of words, like all the words from your favourite books, songs, and conversations. Some words are similar to each other, like "dog" and "puppy," while others are quite different, like "sun" and "ice cream." Word embedding is a technique that enables computers to convert words into numerical representations, allowing them to determine which words are similar or related. But why convert words into numbers? This is because computers don't understand language like we do, so they need to transform words into something they can process—numbers. Thus, word embedding is akin to assigning each word a unique code that computers can decipher. Word embeddings are akin to assigning a unique set of coordinates to every word, creating a vast space that resembles a giant map. On this map, every word gets its own "location" instead of countries or cities. The "location" of each word is represented by a list of values called a vector or word embedding. Computers adjust the vectors based on each word's proximity to work in the training data. Words with similar meanings or that are used similarly are placed close together on the map. Words that are different are far apart. For instance:

"King" might be near "Queen," because they're both royalty.

"Apple" might be near "Banana," because they're both fruits.

"Dog" might be near "Puppy" or "Cat," because they're pets.

"Pizza" would be far from all of the above, but maybe close to "hamburger."

Figure 4.1 shows a highly simplified semantic relationship between words in two dimensions. This is purely for visual illustration purposes, given that machines (and mathematics) enable multiple dimensions of how words are connected or related. The axis, therefore, has no meaning other than to show that we are dealing with a two-dimensional view. Note that some words have arrows linking each other. This is a visual representation of a vector. The second observation that can be made is that similar

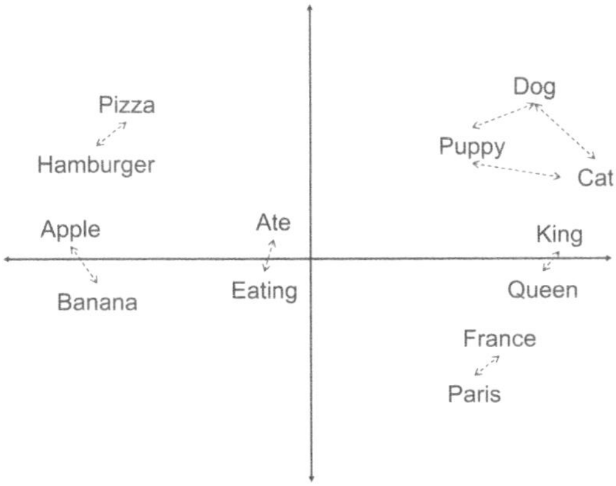

FIGURE 4.1 A highly simplified example of how words are related.

concepts are clustered closer together, or "meaning space." The meaning spaces that are contextually related to each other—e.g. "Ate" and "eating" and the food-related word clusters—have a closer proximity with each other. A third observation is that this technique can also map related concepts such as verb tense and capital-country.

Figure 4.2 presents a three-dimensional visual representation of the word embedding. As can be seen, words related to "love" sit rather closely

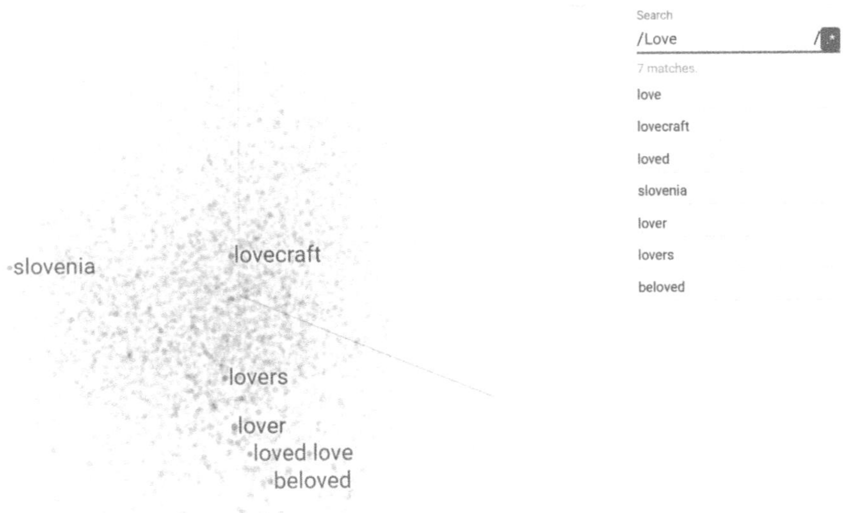

FIGURE 4.2 A three-dimensional representation of word-embedding—"love."

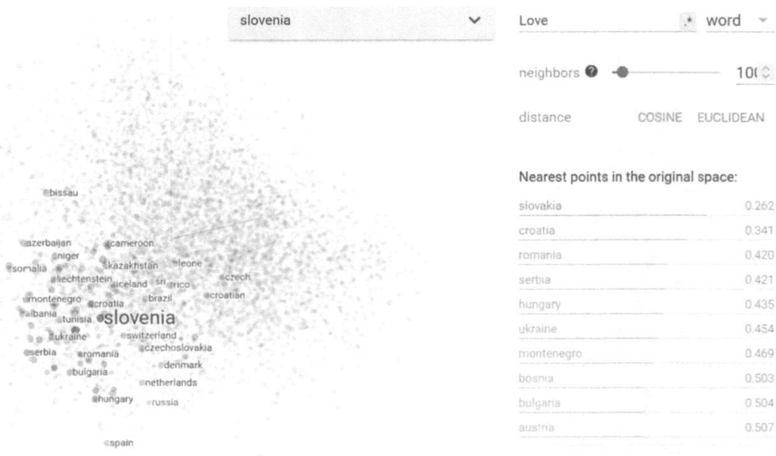

FIGURE 4.3 A three-dimensional representation of word-embedding—"Slovenia."

with each other. The word "Slovenia" is much more distant from the set related to "love." In this case, "Slovenia" is shown because it contains the word "love" but is unrelated to "love." (Sorry to our Slovenian readers. We hope you will be merciful.)

Figure 4.3, on the other hand, shows the words closely related to "Slovenia." Unsurprisingly, as seen on the right-hand side, "Croatia" is one of the words nearest to it, given their cultural similarities and the fact that they are neighbours geographically. But "Slovakia"? We think this is because plenty of documents were used to train the model to compare the differences between the two countries—people often mix up the two if they even know that they are two countries in the first place.

Figure 4.4 shows the word "apries," which is visually very far from the rest of the words. This is again not surprising because apries is a particular, if not rare, word. You probably don't know what it means—and neither do we. At the time of writing, not even Microsoft Word has it in its dictionary. "Apries" is (after looking it up) the fourth Egyptian pharaoh of the 26th dynasty. The idiosyncrasy most likely makes this word a distinct outlier.

In short, word embeddings are dense representations of the individual words in a text, considering the context and other surrounding words with which that particular word occurs.

Two essential points need to be underscored here. Firstly, what has been presented so far is based on a traditional AI technique called natural language processing (NLP). As demonstrated here, computers can determine

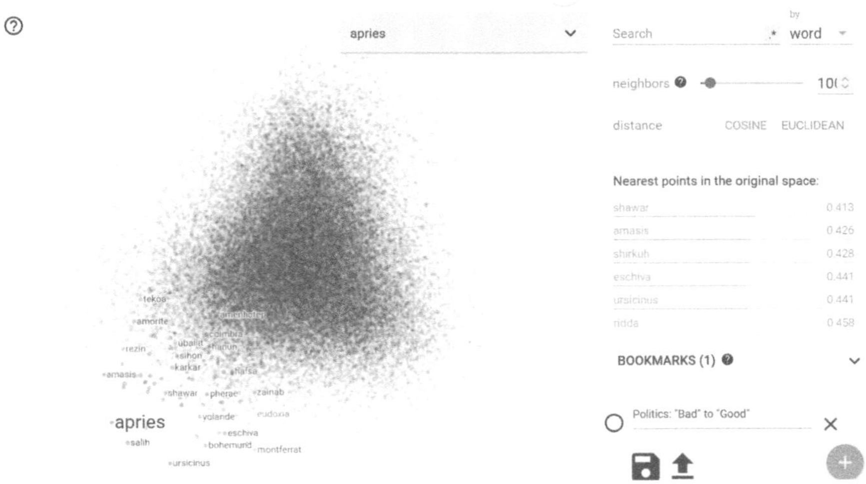

FIGURE 4.4 A three-dimensional representation of word-embedding—“apries.”

the context by analysing the relationship (correlation, to be more precise) between one word and its neighbouring ones. Secondly, based on this NLP approach, if we were able to deploy an enormous set of training data, such as these sentences containing the word “run” above, with enough data, the model would eventually have a significantly higher probability of spotting a pattern that guesses the next best word option in a sequence. Using an enormous amount of words and sentences in a language to assemble a model gives rise to the LLM, the technology behind the likes of ChatGPT. Consequently, the LLM deploys an “attention network” to make connections between different parts of the request/query—commonly known as the “prompt”—we make, churning out a set of meaningful words related to “run.”

ATTENTION IS ALL YOU NEED

So far, so NLP. What we discussed so far pertains to “generative” and “pre-trained.” Let’s now spend some time on how the machine reads words. The emergence of today’s GenAI stems from how machines read words. Before the arrival of the transformer, machines read sentences by scanning each word in a sentence and processing it sequentially like that shown in **Figure 4.5**.

In this case, the machine reads “I” and the words that come after sequentially. Next, when reading the word “run,” the machine scans the neighbour to the left and those on the right, one after another, encoding a

FIGURE 4.5 Before the arrival of the "transformer" technique.

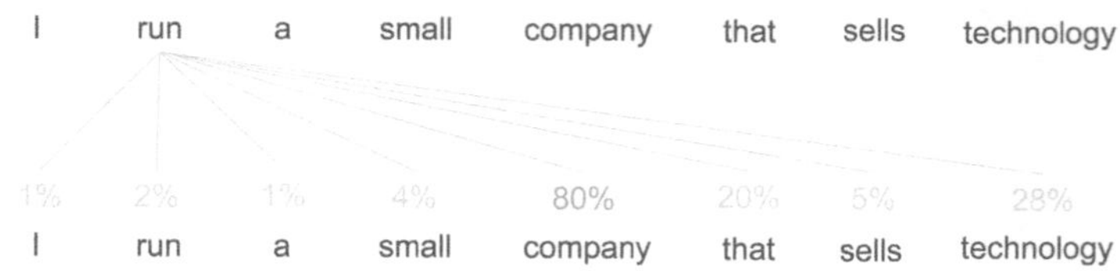

FIGURE 4.6 Figuring out the association by assigning a weight.

value to each word along the way, which is called "weight." We would easily understand the concepts behind the words in this sentence, as shown in **Figure 4.6**. In contrast, an LLM must learn these associations of all the words from the ground up while being trained with billions of language data. In this case, the weight that "run" is assigned to "company" is relatively high (or at least much higher than the rest). The computer would then know the highest probability that what is being run in this context is the company.

Hence, machines understand a language through statistics. Yet, it was the transformer technique that has enabled machines to read and write as fluently as they do today. It radically expanded computers' capabilities to understand language and accelerated the processing speed. Lying at the centre of the transformer is self-attention, which looks at each token in a *body* of text—instead of just a sequence of text—and decides which words are most important to understanding its meaning. Put differently, transformers process an entire sequence, regardless of whether it is parsing a sentence, paragraph or whole article, and analyse all its parts, not just individual words, all in a single moment. Capturing this context gives LLMs far more sophisticated capabilities to parse language. This can be visually presented in **Figure 4.7**.

So, similar to the alien in the film mentioned above, the machine takes a "concept" of the entire sentence instead of working out the meaning by following the words in order. This idea may not be as far-fetched as it

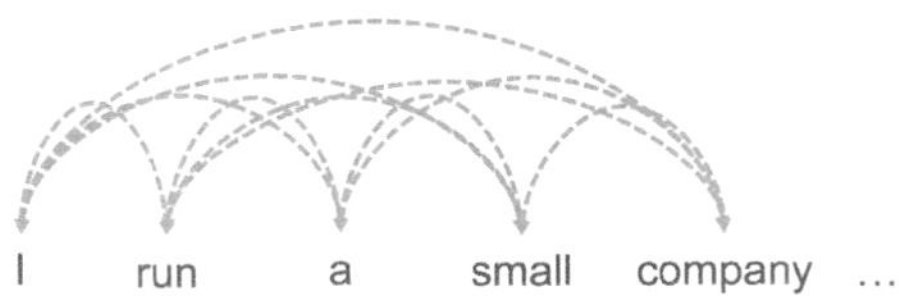

FIGURE 4.7 Reading all the words at the same time.

seems. In English, we use "upgrade" to refer to "the move to a higher level of quality category" in a single word. In German, the word to embark on a train is "einsteigen"—the intention is fully captured in just one word as "ein" means "get into" and "steigen" means "climb." Three of us speak Chinese, a language that can capture ideas using symbols in the form of characters. On many occasions, a single character or two like "孝" can express a profound concept that requires sentences in English to provide even an approximate translation. This Chinese character represents filial piety, which embodies great respect, obedience, care, or even servitude towards one's parents and elders.

Simultaneous processing can significantly accelerate LLM training. More importantly, it enables machines to better understand context and patterns, resulting in more accurate translations and text generation. By focusing on the surrounding text, the model can accurately determine the exact meaning of each word. Consider the following example.

The	dating	app	found	me	a	match	with	whom	I
could	see	a	football	match					
The	dating	app	found	me	a	pairing	with	whom	I
could	see	a	football	game					

The first "match" refers to a romantic partner, whereas the second relates to a competition. The machine recognises this too because it looks at the first use of "match," it places the attention on "dating," "found" and "me." In the second case, "see" and "football" are most attended to by the machine to infer the right meaning. (This is the reason why LLMs and GenAI are always associated with the word "inference"). This functionality is vital for advanced text generation; otherwise, words that can be interchangeable in some contexts can be misused. Hence, the LLM will not make the mistake of confusing the first "match" as "game" or the second as "pairing"—dating to many people may be games but "dating" and "found" are probability-wise less linked to a "game" whereas football "pairing" is uncommon and definitely does not go with "see." A further benefit to this approach is that it helps LLM detect other ambiguities. Consider the following sentence:

Marie put the cake in the fridge because it was hot.

For us humans, we have no problem detecting that the "it" here refers to the cake and not the fridge. So, how does the machine tell? So, we asked an LLM how it managed to catch this, which gave us the following (reasoned) response:

Let me explain how I, as an LLM, analysed this sentence step by step:

1. *First, I identify potential referents:*
    - *"cake"*
    - *"fridge"*
    - *Environmental "it" (from training patterns)*
2. *I look at the structure:*
    - *"Mary put [object1] in [object2] because it was hot"*
3. *I apply semantic knowledge:*
    - *A hot cake makes sense (common)*
    - *A hot fridge is possible but unusual (appliance malfunction)*
    - *Hot weather/environment is very common (everyday usage)*
4. *I use my training patterns:*
    - *I've seen many examples where "it is hot" refers to weather*
    - *Recognizing that putting things in fridges is a common response to hot weather*
    - *Understanding the cause-effect relationship between hot weather and refrigeration*
5. *I assess probability based on training:*
    - *"it was hot" appears frequently in my training as a weather reference*
    - *This pattern matches common usage*

> *However, I should note that I don't actually "recognize" in a human sense - I'm generating responses based on statistical patterns in my training data. When you ask how I recognized it, I'm describing the logical process that my training would suggest, but I don't have true understanding or consciousness of this process as it happens.*

Probability, like traditional AI, is the primary driver of obtaining the correct answer. At their core, LLMs are sophisticated pattern recognition systems trained on vast amounts of text data. Think of them as voracious readers who have consumed billions of documents, from scientific papers to social media posts. However, LLMs do not require labelling or categorisation of content, unlike traditional machine learning techniques. However, this training method creates a fundamental limitation that company executives must be aware of. While these models can generate impressively human-like text, they do not truly "understand" what users want in the way a human assistant would. Consider this critical insight: LLMs do not answer questions; they generate text in response to the prompts they receive.

THE IMPOSSIBLE TRIANGLE OF AI MODELS

If you are familiar with blockchain, you might have encountered the term "blockchain trilemma." This concept outlines the fundamental challenge of achieving three essential elements of blockchain technology—security, scalability, and decentralisation—all at once. Focusing on security often complicates the ability to scale and decentralise. Scalability involves managing a high volume of transactions swiftly and efficiently while keeping transaction costs and times low. However, this focus can hinder the ability to maintain security and decentralisation. Decentralisation signifies an equal distribution of control among all participants rather than being concentrated in a single central entity. Yet, in such a framework without a central authority, maintaining low-cost scaling and robust security becomes problematic.

In the rapidly evolving field of LLMs, we often grapple with a similar "impossible triangle"—the trade-off between accuracy, cost-efficiency, and general purpose. Unlike the blockchain trilemma, where gaining on one front comes at the expense of the others, the LLM triangle suggests that achieving two advantages creates a corresponding disadvantage.

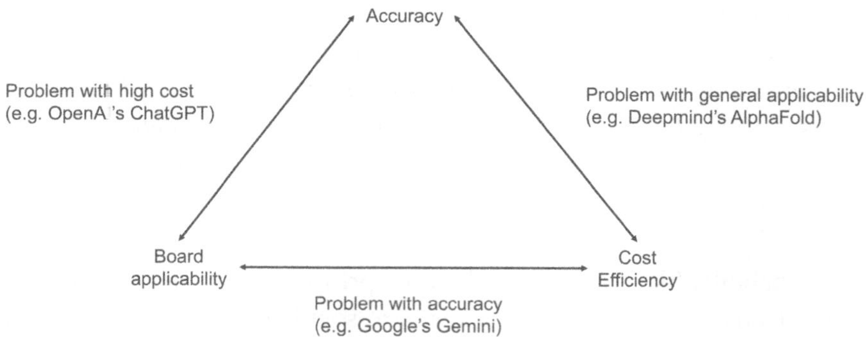

FIGURE 4.3 "The LLM trilemma."

AI practitioners and enthusiasts must understand this trade-off to set realistic expectations and make informed decisions. The impossible triangle is depicted in **Figure 4.8**. Choosing an LLM that excels in accuracy and broad applicability incurs substantial computational and setup costs, as seen with OpenAI's ChatGPT. Conversely, DeepMind, a pioneer in deep learning, developed AlphaFold, which predicts protein structures. Previously, some believed such predictions were impossible. The model succeeded because it was specifically designed to achieve its objectives. However, a model designed for a narrow mission cannot be widely applied to different purposes. Although AlphaFold is not an LLM, it illustrates that highly accurate, cost-effective models typically excel only in narrow, well-defined domains, lacking general-purpose applicability. Additionally, smaller, non-specialised models can manage a wide range of tasks at lower costs, but this often comes at the expense of precision, especially in complex scenarios.

WE ARE SPOILED FOR CHOICE. BUT ARE WE?

AI solution designers may have to make a difficult choice regarding which performance dimension will take a backseat in the "impossible triangle." Indeed, this choice is becoming even harder due to the numerous LLM options available. At the time of writing, there are multiple GenAI suppliers, including industry giants such as Meta and Alphabet, as well as newcomers like Anthropic, Mistral, and Falcon. The market is so crowded now that there is currently no sign of data-rich corporations like Bloomberg and JPMorgan Chase, which have previously expressed an intention to enter the fray.[3] This is perhaps due to the prohibitive development cost. Even Apple and Amazon have yet to join the competition.

Perhaps for precisely this reason, all LLM providers are now competing to be the top choice for solution developers in GenAI. OpenAI's introduction of a straightforward tool for creating ChatGPT-powered apps during its "dev day" in 2024 was likely an attempt to consolidate its position by attracting more users. Recently, ChatGPT also launched a deep research feature and GPT-4.5, while Google offers NotebookLLM, both of which target researchers. ChatGPT is investing significantly in developing models for various purposes, such as o1 for advanced reasoning and o3-mini-high for coding and logic. This is a race to acclimate users to one system, building inertia to encourage continued use in future endeavours. With the highest number of subscribed users in the market, OpenAI is likely in the best position to establish an ecosystem — and create a competitive advantage as a result. That said, solution developers are likely to avoid swearing allegiance to any LLM maker, keeping the option open for selecting GenAI for different projects. This, in turn, has given rise to toolkits such as LangChain, an open-source platform designed to enable users to work across different GenAI systems simultaneously.

The competition at play between different GenAI companies, in many ways, resembles the early days of the duel between iOS and Android. A large ecosystem would enable OpenAI to remain the market leader for a few years until its rivals can join forces. This does not necessarily mean Apple and Google would unite to compete with Microsoft, a partner (read: investor) to OpenAI. We would likely see rivals agreeing on the same standard to collaborate against OpenAI's dominance. We believe this is not dissimilar to the situation in 2015 in which Android's supporters finally established a meaningful ecosystem to rival iOS. As the LLM market consolidates, we may have two or three large factions competing. Expect more big tech and startup companies to redouble their efforts to be at the heart of these systems.

This narrative would probably have continued for a while had DeepSeek not made an appearance. In early 2025, the Chinese start-up shocked the LLM world—along with investors making big bets on them—with a far more efficient model that performs almost as well as ChatGPT, but was trained at a fraction of the cost. This is primarily attributable to its efficient architecture (more on this in a later chapter). However, what has far wider applications in business, at least, is the fact that it is open-source. (Meta's LLM Llama also claims to be "open-source" but DeepSeek is far more open, with almost all the code freely downloadable). The result is that companies have already opted to test and run their AI solutions using the Chinese-made LLM.[4] The "Sputnik" moment is not only a wake-up call to the LLM makers, who have been pouring massive amounts of money into developments, but it also signifies a change in market dynamics. Will these outfits be able to recuperate their investments in the future? How will companies react to such market evolution? To answer this question, one must first examine how they have utilised GenAI.

NOTES

1 Murgia, Madhumita (2024) *Code Dependent: Living in the Shadow of AI.* London: Picador.

2 Vaswani, Ashish, Shazeer, Noam, Parmar, Niki, Uszkoreit, Jakob, Jones, Llion, Gomez, Aidan N., Kaiser, Lukasz and Polosukhin, Illia (2017) "Attention is all you need," *arxiv*, https://arxiv.org/abs/1706.03762.

3 CB Insights (2023) *Generative AI Bible: The Ultimate Guide to GenAI Disruption*, November 7.

4 The Economist (2025) "Western companies are experimenting with DeepSeek," March 13, https://www.economist.com/business/2025/03/13/western-companies-are-experimenting-with-deepseek. Accessed on 27 March 2025.

CHAPTER 5

Current and Future Trajectories of GenAI

THE LAUNCH OF CHATGPT in November 2022 has not only sparked imagination but also promised the emergence of numerous new and expansive opportunities. Since then, there has been no shortage of reminders that generative AI (GenAI) is poised to transform entire sectors of the economy, from creative work[1] to customer experience,[2] while reshaping, if not eliminating, millions of jobs worldwide. On this last point, a recent study revealed that within a few months of ChatGPT's launch, copywriters and graphic designers on major online freelancing platforms experienced a sharp decline in the number of jobs they secured, accompanied by an even steeper drop in earnings. This indicated that GenAI was not only taking away their work but also devaluing the work they continued to perform.[3]

On the positive side, another experiment revealed that participants assigned to use ChatGPT were more productive and efficient and found the tasks more enjoyable. Participants with weaker skills benefited the most from ChatGPT, suggesting that those with less highly skilled workforces typically achieved the most significant performance gains. GenAI's nature may have a particularly significant impact on the production of writing and graphics. How about other lines of work that require broader knowledge? In another study, some consultants have been randomly assigned to carry out a set of tasks using ChatGPT-4. It was found that GenAI-assisted staff were far more productive than their unassisted colleagues. Not only did GenAI-empowered consultants undertake their tasks 25% faster and

DOI: 10.1201/9781003559665-5

complete 12% more tasks overall, but their work was also judged to be 40% higher in quality than that produced by peers who did not access the tool.[4]

Not surprisingly, consulting firms have rushed to offer strategic advice to their clients on the best ways to harness the power of GenAI. Investment banks are keen to share their enthusiasm for investing in GenAI, churning out report after report. And then there are numerous projections on where GenAI will take us. We have been warned to expect chatbots that can hold proper conversations.[5] We have also been informed that chatbots can resolve up to 75% of customer issues.[6] Even more impressive is that we can build GenAI-driven chatbots in under an hour![7] To put all these in a straightforward message: GenAI is coming to town, fast—and eating our lunch!

If GenAI chatbots can confer numerous advantages and can be built easily and quickly, why have we not seen widespread and rapid adoption by businesses by now? Indeed, companies have been attempting to embrace this new technology. Yet, the pace is significantly slower than anticipated and, indeed, not as swift as the media would suggest. Clearly, utilising GenAI in business is not as straightforward as it seems. This chapter highlights some of the latest developments in the GenAI space. We begin by mapping out the value and supply chain of the GenAI industry. Building upon the insights from the preceding chapter, we endeavour to present a comprehensive picture that reveals the complex network of stakeholders, processes, and resources that constitutes the backbone of today's GenAI technology. Subsequently, it discusses the constraints and challenges that may hinder the development and broader adoption of GenAI technology. By shedding light on these critical barriers, we aim to foster a deeper understanding of the complexities that shape the progress of GenAI and its future. By exploring these multifaceted challenges, we can gain a more nuanced understanding of why the adoption of GenAI in business settings may be slower than initially anticipated. This deeper insight into the complexities of implementation provides a foundation for developing more realistic strategies to leverage GenAI's potential while addressing the associated hurdles.

THE VALUE CHAIN OF GENAI

Any GenAI user will tell you that leveraging the power of AI is easy enough these days. And you can do it for free. Such easy and frictionless access could have easily led us to overvalue the benefits that GenAI can yield and under-estimate the difficulties in fashioning it into true business

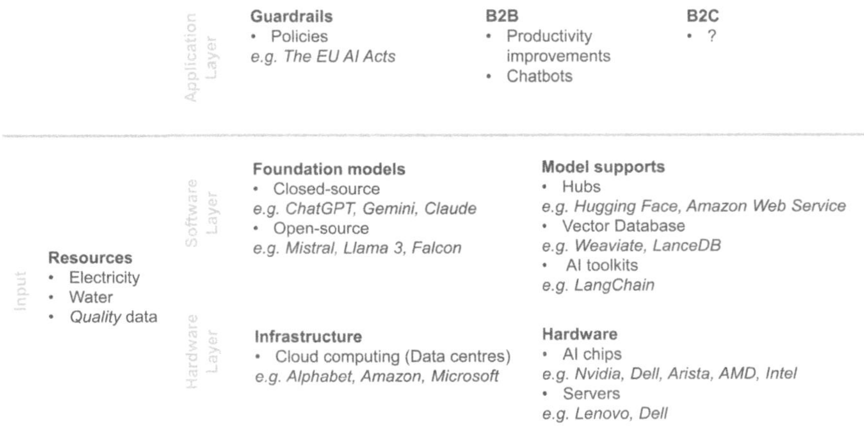

FIGURE 5.1 A highly simplified view of the GenAI value chain.

propositions. To understand where GenAI is heading—and where it is leading us—is to see how the various components in the value chain that bring GenAI forward are developing and interacting with each other. **Figure 5.1** offers a highly simplified view of the value chain.

Let's start with the "input"—the fundamental elements behind all AI technologies. The primary assertion here is that with the insatiable demand for developing more advanced GenAI, these elements are under enormous pressure. The trouble is so severe that IBM has called these crises.[8] The first is the energy problem. Companies creating the large language models (LLMs) require more power each year, and our current energy infrastructure is finding it increasingly difficult to meet the demand. According to some estimates, the amount of electricity required to train OpenAI's GPT-3 is enough to drive a car to the moon and back, or enough to power 126 households in Denmark for a year.[9] The considerably larger GPT-4, which will have many more characteristics than the previous generation, would certainly require far more power to train. The water needed to cool servers is another natural resource in high demand. It was also calculated that 700,000 litres of fresh water had been needed for training GPT-3, which is comparable to producing 320 Tesla cars.[10] GenAI may be beneficial, but it is not necessarily environmentally friendly or sustainable. The energy and water consumption required for training and running LLMs is not merely an environmental concern; it is also a significant economic and logistical challenge for both companies and governments. As models increase in size and complexity, alongside the growing number of new models emerging, all of this will come at the expense of maintaining the infrastructures and systems necessary to ensure a steady supply of water and electricity.

There may be an upside to all these. The substantial energy requirements are driving innovation in green computing technologies. Companies are increasingly exploring renewable energy sources to power their data centres and investigating novel cooling technologies to reduce water consumption. Some organisations are even considering locating their AI infrastructure in regions with abundant renewable energy sources and cooler climates to minimise both energy consumption and cooling needs. The massive computational requirements of GenAI are pushing companies to have better data centre design and management. Traditional data centre cooling solutions are struggling to keep up with the heat generated by dense clusters of AI processors, leading to innovations in liquid cooling and other advanced thermal management techniques. This has created new opportunities for companies specialising in data centre infrastructure, from cooling system manufacturers to power management firms. It's also driving research into novel computing paradigms, such as quantum computing and neuromorphic hardware, which promise to overcome some of the limitations of traditional silicon-based processors. Electronic waste created by rapidly obsolete hardware is also a problem, and there are calls for more sustainable practices. This has led to an increased focus on developing more energy-efficient AI algorithms and hardware, as well as exploring alternative materials and manufacturing processes. Some companies are also investing in circular economy initiatives, aiming to extend the lifespan of AI hardware and improve recycling processes for electronic components.

Another issue raised is that data is about to run out, at least the quality ones. The vast troves of data used to train LLMs are being depleted. GenAI is trained on data available on the Internet, and the supply of high-quality language data is expected to be exhausted between 2026 and 2035.[11] Nevertheless, man-made (or machine-made, to be more precise) data can partially alleviate this problem. Indeed, data is generated with every movement and action we take. Hence, it is rather the tools for capturing the data that cannot keep pace with LLM data training than the data itself. It's also important to note that, to enhance GenAI's capabilities, greater human involvement will be necessary. Most real-world problems—from running a business to being an effective doctor—are complex and lack clear-cut solutions or definable, measurable objectives. Therefore, in such intricate domains, data to train models is still required from individuals who can distinguish between good- and bad-quality responses. Anecdotally, Terence and Mark have been receiving requests to help utilise their subject expertise to guide LLMs in producing more precise and relevant results. All of this, in turn, is bound to slow things down.

INFRASTRUCTURE AND HARDWARE

Like all computing technologies, GenAI requires both hardware and software. With LLM producers needing space for data and companies needing to secure and run their own data, cloud computing and data centres have been thriving—and very profitable—businesses. According to one estimate, global demand for data centre capability could more than triple by 2030[12]—various hardware must be used in conjunction with data centre infrastructure. First and foremost are AI chips, which are critical for powering GenAI. Its demand has, for a long time, far outstripped supply, leading to a bottleneck, especially for the top-performing ones. But this problem seems to be receiving relief, with lead time by market leader Nvidia narrowing as more and more competitors join the fray. However, the future development is a question mark. In September 2022, the CEO of Nvidia declared that "Moore's Law is dead" to AI chips, referring to the law that the cost for the same level of computer performance is halved every two years.[13] As LLM developers strive to secure the best-performing AI chips, prices are expected to continue rising. This, in turn, means that the cost of training ever-larger foundation models will continue to creep up. The strategic importance of AI hardware has elevated it to a matter of national security for many countries. The global chip shortage and concerns about supply chain resilience have prompted governments to invest heavily in domestic semiconductor manufacturing capabilities. These dynamics have led to a complex geopolitical landscape, with countries vying for technological supremacy and implementing policies to protect their AI hardware industries. Furthermore, the concentration of advanced AI chip manufacturing capabilities within a handful of companies and countries has raised concerns about potential monopolies and the necessity for diversification in the supply chain. This situation has spurred efforts to develop open-source hardware designs and foster a more diverse ecosystem of AI chip manufacturers.

Other hardware suppliers have also benefited from the AI boom. For instance, Lenovo, the world's largest manufacturer of personal computers, has seen its revenue grow at its fastest pace in two and a half years. It has now positioned itself to benefit from the rollout of AI servers.[14] The rapid advancement of GenAI has spurred innovation in chip design and architecture. Traditional chip manufacturers are now competing with specialised AI chip designers to create more efficient and powerful processors explicitly tailored for AI workloads. These AI-specific chips, often referred to as Neural Processing Units (NPUs) or Tensor Processing Units (TPUs), are designed to optimise the matrix multiplication operations that form the backbone of many AI algorithms. This specialisation allows for significant improvements in performance and energy efficiency compared to general-purpose processors. Moreover, the push for edge AI—running AI models on local devices rather than in the cloud—is driving the development of low-power, high-performance AI chips for mobile devices, IoT sensors, and other edge computing applications. This trend could potentially alleviate some of the strain on data centre infrastructure while enabling new AI-powered applications in areas with limited connectivity.

While all these problems can lead us to view the future developments of AI in a dim light, there are reasons for more optimism. After all, we still beat a pathway to develop powerful yet efficient GenAI. We have to reach that right point, according to the so-called "scaling hypothesis." This refers to:

> Once we find a scalable architecture which can be applied fairly uniformly, we can simply train ever larger networks and ever more sophisticated behavior will emerge naturally as the easiest way to optimize for all the tasks and data. More powerful NNs (neural networks) are "just" scaled-up weak NNs, in much the same way that human brains look much like scaled-up primate brains.[15]

In short, even if a few incremental technical advances are required on the development path, continuing to train AI models using ever more significant amounts of computational power and data will inevitably lead to human-like AI. On the other hand, sceptics would argue that just because AI systems can produce human-like responses does not necessarily mean they will think like humans. After all, Russell Crowe plays Nobel Prize-winning mathematician John Nash in the 2001 film *A Beautiful Mind*. Nobody would imagine that the better his acting performance, the more impressive his mathematical skills must be. Will the AI models be able to get to human-level reasoning?

FOUNDATION MODELS

At the core of the software layer—and indeed GenAI—are the LLMs. These days, they are often referred to as foundation models. Following the definition given by the Stanford Institute for Human-Centered Artificial Intelligence, such models are "models trained on broad data … recent advances in deep learning and computer systems applied at a huge scale demonstrate surprising emergent capabilities and substantially improve performance on a wide range of downstream tasks."[16] The central idea is that companies can now leverage the flexibility of these foundation models and utilise them as a backbone to build AI solutions specialised in tackling individual issues. The table below summarises at the time of writing the various characteristics of some of the most prominent LLMs.

Model	**Open/Closed***	**Strengths**	**Weaknesses**	**Best For**
ChatGPT	Closed	Conversational fluency, structured responses, strong summarisation and content creation, coding assistance	No real-time web access, limited multimodal capabilities (text-only), privacy concerns due to data storage	SEO, copywriting, advertising, summarisation, coding assistance
Llama 3.3	Open	Open-source accessibility, cost-efficient self-hosting, multilingual support, domain adaptability	Slightly weaker in complex reasoning and safety alignment compared to proprietary models	Customised AI solutions, research and development, edge/offline applications
Gemini 2.5 Pro	Closed	Real-time web access, multimodal capabilities (images/videos), massive 1M token context window for reasoning	Struggles with mathematical reasoning involving large numbers, aggressive content filtering	Academic research, enterprise applications requiring large context windows
DeepSeek-R1	Open (MIT License)	Strong reasoning and coding performance, cost-efficient MoE architecture	Slightly weaker English proficiency compared to proprietary models	Open-source development, research applications
Qwen2.5-Max	Open	Mathematical reasoning, coding proficiency, multilingual support	Requires higher computational resources for deployment	Enterprise applications, gaming systems

(Continued)

Model	Open/Closed*	Strengths	Weaknesses	Best For
Falcon LLM	Open	Lightweight efficiency for domain-specific tasks	Limited model sizes compared to competitors; struggles with dialogue generation	Lightweight applications, domain-specific AI solutions
Mistral Large 2	Open for research, Closed for commercial use	Code generation, mathematics, reasoning, multilingual support (13+ languages), 128K token context window, function calling, efficient single-node inference	Not fully open-source, requires commercial licensing for professional use, slightly lower performance in some benchmarks compared to larger models	Research, commercial deployment (via IBM watsonx), coding assistance, mathematical problem-solving, multilingual applications

* Open-source LLMS offer flexibility for customisation and further fine-tuning, whereas closed-source ones often come with proprietary restrictions but offer polished, high-quality outputs suitable for professional applications

As of March 2025. *Sources:* https://meetcody.ai/blog/falcon-llm-180b-40b-open-source-ai/; https://pynomial.com/2025/02/03-mini-vs-deepseek-r1-vs-qwen-llm/; https://www.linkedin.com/pulse/qwen-25-alibabas-breakthrough-open-source-ai-dmitry-shapiro-8tepc; https://botpenguin.com/blogs/falcon-llm-vs-other-language-models; https://www.voiceflow.com/blog/deepseek; https://infermatic.ai/ask/?question=What+are+the+strengths+and+weaknesses+of+Qwen+language+models%3F

As mentioned in the previous chapters, AI has been little more than a highly efficient machine designed to perform a single task to the best degree possible. Even today, most AI business solutions must be tailor-made to reach their expected level of usefulness. Companies that want to use AI to automate the data extraction of, say, bank statements and driver's licenses must build and deploy two separate AI solutions. This, in turn, requires companies to accumulate enough—often a large amount of—data to train each model to attain an acceptable level of model accuracy.

LLMs offer two possibilities that traditional AI don't provide. Firstly, they are like flexible, recyclable AI that can be reused for different purposes. Secondly, individuals and companies will no longer need to build AI models from scratch, as foundation models already trained on a massive dataset can be utilised. LLMs can be used straight out of the box. We can plug-and-play GenAI, much like picking up a telephone to make calls. Undoubtedly, many of us have experienced in, if not already an avid user of, the likes of ChatGPT. All it takes to use them is merely *prompting* or *prompt engineering*—giving commands and requests to LLMs and receiving answers to our queries without the need to supplement any new data. Asking the right questions can help accomplish various tasks, including text summarisation, information extraction, question answering, text classification, conversation, code generation, and reasoning.

For businesses, however, capitalising on the power of LLMs requires a more nuanced approach. This is not least because companies often have more complex and diverse needs. This, in turn, means that more work will be required to achieve optimal performance using GenAI as a foundation model. While the plug-and-play nature of LLMs offers tremendous potential, businesses are discovering that harnessing their full power often requires significant customisation and integration efforts. Companies are increasingly exploring ways to fine-tune these models with domain-specific data to improve their performance in specialised tasks. For instance, in the healthcare sector, LLMs are being adapted to understand medical terminology and assist in diagnosis. However, this requires careful curation of medical datasets and collaboration with healthcare professionals to ensure accuracy and compliance with regulations. Similarly, in the legal industry, LLMs are being tailored to interpret complex legal language and assist in document review, but this necessitates extensive training on legal precedents and jurisdictional nuances.

Implementing LLMs in business environments also raises important questions about data privacy and security. Companies must carefully consider how to leverage these powerful models without compromising sensitive information. This has led to the development of techniques like federated learning, where models are trained on decentralised data without directly accessing it, and differential privacy, which adds noise to data to protect individual privacy while maintaining overall utility. Moreover, the interpretability and explainability of LLM outputs can pose significant challenges in business contexts, particularly in regulated industries where decision-making processes must be transparent and auditable. This has spurred research into methods for making AI decision-making more understandable and accountable. Companies, therefore, need to gain a more nuanced understanding of how businesses are navigating the complexities of LLM implementation, balancing the promise of out-of-the-box functionality with the need for customisation and responsible AI practices.

Retrieval-Augmented Generation

One of the biggest problems with GenAI is hallucinations, which refer to instances where GenAI produces outputs that are factually incorrect, nonsensical or even downright misleading and wrong while presenting them as credible and accurate. This is why many LLMs include a disclaimer such as "ChatGPT can make mistakes. Check important info" or "Gemini can make mistakes, including about people. So, double-check it." Companies, therefore, need to find ways to incorporate company-specific knowledge into their AI outputs. The so-called retrieval-augmented generation (RAG) has recently emerged as a powerful intermediate solution. This approach bridges the gap between general AI capabilities and specialised organisational needs by connecting AI models to proprietary data sources. RAG enables AI systems to reference and utilise internal documentation, policies, and expertise while generating responses.

To use an analogy, consider RAG as a Michelin-starred kitchen run by a master chef. The chef possesses two essential tools: years of culinary expertise, similar to the LLM's trained knowledge, and a comprehensive digital recipe library that functions as a retrieval system. When a VIP guest requests a custom dish, the chef does not depend solely on memory or existing knowledge, which could lead to inconsistencies; neither does she replicate an existing recipe, which would lack creativity. Instead, she first consults the library for relevant recipes, techniques, and ingredient combinations. She then combines this new knowledge with her culinary expertise to create something unique that fulfils the VIP guest's specific requests. Like a masterful dish that integrates proven techniques with innovative interpretation, RAG merges retrieved factual information with advanced generation capabilities to produce accurate and contextually appropriate responses. The result is a perfectly executed dish that balances established knowledge with creative adaptation—precise, reliable, and highly tailored to current needs. The implementation of RAG involves several key components working in harmony. At its core, RAG utilises a retrieval system, typically based on vector embeddings, to search and retrieve relevant information from a company's knowledge base. This retrieval process is often powered by sophisticated semantic search algorithms that can understand the context and intent of queries, going beyond simple keyword matching. Once relevant information is retrieved, it is then fed into the language model along with the original query. This process, known as "context injection," enables the model to generate responses grounded in specific, up-to-date information while leveraging its general language understanding capabilities.

One of the primary advantages of RAG is its ability to keep AI responses current and factual without requiring constant retraining of the entire model. This is particularly valuable in fast-changing environments where information quickly becomes outdated. However, implementing RAG is not without challenges. It requires careful curation and maintenance of the knowledge base to ensure the retrieved information is accurate and relevant. Organisations must also consider the cost of computing and running both retrieval and generation processes in real time, which can impact response times. As RAG technology matures, we can expect to see more sophisticated retrieval mechanisms that can handle multimodal data, including text, images, and audio. This could enable AI systems to provide more comprehensive and nuanced responses by drawing on a broader range of information sources. There's also growing interest in developing more dynamic and adaptive RAG systems. These could potentially learn from user interactions to improve both retrieval accuracy and the relevance of generated responses over time, creating a continuously evolving knowledge ecosystem within organisations. By delving deeper into these aspects of RAG, we gain a more comprehensive understanding of its potential to revolutionise how businesses leverage AI while maintaining control over their proprietary knowledge and ensuring contextually appropriate outputs.

Fine-Tuning

Fine-tuning represents the most sophisticated approach for companies requiring highly specialised AI capabilities. This method involves customising the AI model's training on specific datasets, enabling it to develop deep expertise in particular domains. Both RAG and fine-tuning have now become a centre-stage training process for foundation models. Think of fine-tuning as the difference between having a brilliant new employee with encyclopaedic knowledge (LLM), guided and instructed by a seasoned professional who knows the industry, company culture, and specifics to accomplish an objective (fine-tuning). Hence, companies can leverage a pre-trained base model by introducing specialised data to update the model's parameters to complete a task. Suppose we want to create AI Terence, AI Mark, AI Danny and AI Paul to talk like the human versions of Terence, Mark, Danny and Paul, respectively. In this case, it is possible to layer the LLMs with data on the speaking style and choice of words of each of these (tragically egoistic and unbearably self-important) humans. (A fact: Terence, Mark, Danny and Paul all think it is nothing short of an excellent contribution to humankind….) Undoubtedly, this represents a giant leap forward in reaching those business objectives that previously companies could not attain due to a lack of sufficiently large amounts of data or AI model builders. Yet, full fine-tuning has heavy demands that hinder practical and easy adoption across businesses. These demands include intensive memory needs. As the size of LLMs continues to grow, with the most prominent models now reaching hundreds of gigabytes, the memory requirements for full fine-tuning are becoming prohibitive. Another problem with full fine-tuning is that it can suffer from the so-called "catastrophic forgetting" problem. As it turns out, fine-tuning a new task on an existing LLM can lead previous knowledge to be overwritten or forgotten. Put differently, fine-tuning for a new task may come to the detriment of the performance of previously trained tasks. This issue makes it difficult to adapt a foundation model to multiple tasks. Lastly, creating a foundation model to tackle a diverse range of tasks requires ever-increasing storage and computational costs.

To overcome these problems, efforts have been made to combine both tuning and prompting, a technique known as parameter-efficient fine-tuning (PEFT). PEFT allows for task-specific adjustments without incurring the full cost of retraining. We will highlight two approaches to illustrate how they work: prompt tuning and low-rank adaptation (LoRA). For the former, imagine you are playing a video game with a character with many abilities and skills. Still, you need the character to perform a special move perfect for a particular game level. PEFT, in this case, is akin to giving your character specific instructions for the level. It does not involve changing anything about the character's abilities. Instead, you provide precise instructions, such as "use only a shotgun, stay low, and keep moving." Prompting the character in this way helps it focus on the right tactics without altering the fundamentals of the character. In other words, prompt tuning is like telling the characters *how* to play the level differently without upgrading their skills. In contrast, LoRA is similar to adding a temporary gadget that improves the character's performance in the game level. Instead of changing your character's primary abilities, you temporarily give them a new gadget—like night vision goggles, a camouflage cloak or a flamethrower—just for this level. The character retains all its built-in skills but is now enhanced with this new, specific tool. In summary, while resource-intensive, fine-tuning offers the highest degree of customisation and can produce exceptional results for specialised applications. The key to successful AI enhancement lies in adopting a systematic, stepped approach. Businesses should view these methods as a progression ladder, starting with the most straightforward solutions and advancing only when necessary. Companies can develop a customised solution that aligns with their specific needs and resources by understanding and strategically implementing these three approaches—prompt engineering, RAG, and fine-tuning. The key lies in starting simple and scaling up complexity only as required, ensuring efficient resource use while maximising the value derived from AI systems.

MODEL SUPPORTS

As powerful as it appears and as human-like as its response seems, GenAI by itself does not produce much value. To turn LLMs into practical GenAI solutions, these models must be used in conjunction with and supported by other tools, all in addition to the necessary infrastructure and hardware. First and foremost, there are hubs, which is another way to calling a library that developers can tap. Companies operating in this space include Hugging Face and Amazon Web Services. The former, for instance, provides pre-trained models for text generation, translation, and sentiment analysis. This simplifies the process of integrating complex ML models into applications. The company also hosts a vast repository of over 30,000 datasets that users can leverage to train their models. This includes data for various tasks across NLP, computer vision, and audio processing.[17,18] In addition to these, users can share their models and datasets openly. Another kind of support is the vector database. Two companies that offer this service are LanceDB and Weaviate. According to the website of the latter at least, it claims that the service provided would reduce hallucination (recall that GenAI can fabricate output) by acting as the data sources for RAG (remember that is a validation technique that improves GenAI's ability to speak the truth), data leakage (when a model uses data during training that would not be available at the time of prediction, which, in turn, causes a model to look accurate until deployed), and vendor lock-in (many developers are unwilling to be locked in by any of the LLM providers and to retain the option of being able to select different LLM for different projects).[19] LangChain, on the other hand, is an AI toolkit provider that helps developers adopt LLMs. For example, it offers building blocks and application programming interfaces (APIs) to integrate LLMs into a solution.[20]

APPLICATION LAYERS

This is where things become truly interesting—harnessing GenAI technologies to sell to other businesses (B2B) and directly to consumers (B2C). While these will be the focus of the next chapters, regulatory guardrails also extend into the application layer. The EU AI Act, published in June 2023, is the world's first comprehensive AI law. Included within it are new rules addressing the level of risk posed by AI for providers and users. The EU identifies the following as "unacceptable risks," referring to systems deemed threatening to people, which will be banned. They include::

- Cognitive behavioural manipulation of people or specific vulnerable groups, e.g. voice-activated toys that encourage dangerous behaviour in children;
- Social scoring, i.e. classifying people based on behaviour, socio-economic status or personal characteristics;
- Biometric identification and categorisation of people; and
- Real-time and remote biometric identification systems, such as facial recognition

It is worth noting that some exceptions may be permitted for the purposes of law enforcement. "High risk" involves AI systems that negatively affect safety or fundamental rights. It is divided into two categories:

a. AI systems used in products falling under the EU's product safety legislation. This includes toys, aviation, cars, medical devices and lifts;

b. AI systems falling into specific areas that will have to be registered in an EU database, including:
    - Management and operation of critical infrastructure
    - Education and vocational training
    - Employment, worker management and access to self-employment
    - Access to and enjoyment of essential private services and public services and benefits
    - Law enforcement

- Migration, asylum and border control management
- Assistance in legal interpretation and application of the law

All high-risk AI systems will be assessed before being made available in the market and throughout their lifecycle. The public can file complaints about AI systems to designated national authorities.

Transparency requirements are another consideration. While GenAI will not be classified as high-risk above, it must comply with transparency requirements and EU copyright law by:

- Disclosing that the content was generated by AI
- Designing the model to prevent it from generating illegal content
- Publishing summaries of copyrighted data used for training

Content that is either generated or modified by AI, such as deepfake images, audio, or video files, must be clearly labelled as AI-generated so that users are aware when they encounter such content. It is also believed that more advanced LLMs may pose systemic risk. Therefore, they would have to undergo thorough evaluations (although the exact meaning of this is unclear at the time of writing). Last but not least, the Act aims at *supporting innovation.* It offers start-ups and small- to medium-sized enterprises opportunities to develop and train AI models before releasing them to the general public. National authorities will, therefore, be required to provide companies with a testing environment that simulates conditions close to the real world.

B2B AND B2C: THE USE CASE CRISIS

This is where the big question mark arises. Despite all the hype and media frenzy, GenAI's potential value in both B2B and B2C spaces has fallen far short of expectations. So much so that the IBM report mentioned earlier argues that GenAI has yet to find its "killer app" in the enterprise context, referring to it as a "use case crisis. "Some pessimistic critics have suggested that future applications might not meaningfully extend beyond "parlour trick" status. This crisis has also been dubbed the "$600 billion question."[21] By considering the amount of investment made in AI infrastructure spending for a quick back-of-the-envelope calculation, a prominent venture capital firm suggests that $600 billion is the minimum AI revenue needed to justify and repay the massive upfront investments the market has made.[22] So, despite the substantial amounts being channelled into AI investments, why are predictions consistently missing the mark? Why does the elusive "killer app" remain just that—elusive? The answer perhaps lies in three fundamental truths about the technological revolution that we repeatedly seem to forget.

The Perpetual Challenge of Prediction

History is filled with exuberant technological predictions that have failed to materialise. This lays bare our inability to accurately predict the impact of technology. This goes beyond Peter Thiel's famous saying, "We wanted flying cars, instead we got 140 characters." The 1980s witnessed similar concerns about the Walkman, with fears that it would turn people into "wind-up non-humans." The legislation attempted to ban headphone use in public spaces, and one New Jersey resident even faced potential imprisonment for asserting his right to walk while wearing headphones.[23] Our track record of technological prediction is, quite simply, abysmal.

The Reality of Technology Diffusion

The second truth is more sobering: meaningful technology diffusion invariably requires time. Technologies often begin with relatively few applications—significant uses emerge only much later. Television started by filming people on stage. Streaming entertainment developed only many decades afterwards. The Internet began as a method for file sharing before evolving into the web. WhatsApp, Uber, and TikTok also arrived much later. Similarly, the actual value and benefits of GenAI become apparent only when businesses engage with it over an extended period across various functions to pursue different goals. The killer apps in this area will take time for businesses to uncover. Consider also the computer revolution—its first two decades yielded negligible productivity gains. Electric machinery followed a similar trajectory, requiring 15 to 20 years to demonstrate substantial impact.[24] Our own experience at Nexus FrontierTech may provide additional insight. Since founding the company in 2017, we have worked to help organisations adopt AI. However, it was not until late 2024 that we began to witness widespread openness to AI technologies—and even then, this openness does not necessarily extend beyond proofs of concept and translate into implementation. Given these observations, what we are experiencing now might be less about the AI revolution and more about a "get-rich-quick" illusion fuelled by GPU stockpiling.

The Ecosystem Requirement

Transformative technologies do not operate in isolation. As economic historian Carlota Perez aptly observes, "a revolutionary technology is not the same thing as a technological revolution."[25] A historical analysis of major technological revolutions—from the industrial revolution of the 1770s to the IT revolution of the 1980s—reveals that true transformation necessitates concurrent evolution in governmental and societal structures, often resulting in new institutions like trade unions, regulatory bodies, and welfare systems. In other words, revolutionary technologies require revolutionary ecosystems—comprehensive environments that can support and sustain transformative change. While the substantial investments in AI emphasise the technology's perceived potential, history and current realities indicate that realising this potential will require patience and systemic change. The AI revolution is not solely about deploying new technology but fundamentally reshaping how we organise, operate, and conceptualise business and society.

From our front-seat rows in helping companies adopt and use AI, we see many struggling. Many businesses, regardless of their size, still struggle to integrate traditional AI into their operations. For them, GenAI can be complex, and at least it is geared to serve specific purposes. While it can write a 5,000-word report in no time, it cannot, for example, perform a basic data entry task, such as extracting and classifying driver's license data, which traditional AI can do easily. As such, companies need to think deeply and carefully about which business cases might be appropriate in their search for GenAI gold. Navigating traditional AI is like steaming through choppy waters with a state-of-the-art but somewhat cumbersome vessel. GenAI, in many ways, adds more tonnage and power, creating a more turbulent sea. A company still unsteady with the former may struggle with the latter. As hard as it is, it still makes sense for companies to forge a path forward (even if it can feel like everyone else has it figured out). So, how can businesses tackle the deployment of GenAI in their operations? This is what we will address in the next chapter, Chapter 6. Indeed, there is always a question of what lies ahead of GenAI in the long run. In our view, the current stage of the GenAI evolution throws us back to just before the millennium. While companies back then may have seen the need for setting up websites, few could see the specific roles that the wider internet would play as an integral part of omnichannel strategies, let alone across devices and as phone apps. This requires us to look further afield to see what kind of an AI-powered future awaits us when we become AI native, the focus of Chapter 7.

NOTES

1 De Cremer, David, Morini Bianzino, Nicola and Falk, Ben (2023) "How generative AI could disrupt creative work," *Harvard Business Review*, April 13, https://hbr.org/2023/04/how-generative-ai-could-disrupt-creative-work. Accessed on 29 October 2024.

2 Siggelkow, Nicolaj and Terwiesch, Christian (2023) "Create winning customer experiences with generative AI," *Harvard Business Review*, April4,https://hbr.org/2023/04/create-winning-customer-experiences-with-generative-ai. Accessed on 29 October 2024.

3 Noy, Shakked, and Zhang, Whitney (2023) "Experimental evidence on the productivity effects of generative artificial intelligence", *Science*, 381(6654), 13 July, pp. 187–192.

4 Dell'Acqua, Fabrizio, McFowland, Edward III, Mollick, Ethan, Lifshitz-Assaf, Hila, Kellogg, Katherine C., Rajendran, Saran, Krayer, Lisa, Candelon, François and Lakhani, Karim R. (2023) "Navigating the jagged technological frontier: Field experimental evidence of the effects of AI on knowledge worker productivity and quality," *Harvard Business School Working Paper*, Working Paper 24-013. Accessed on 31 October 2024.

5 Ball, Max (2024) *Get Ready for GenAI Chatbots: The State of Conversational AI*, October 7, https://www.forrester.com/blogs/get-ready-for-genai-chatbots-the-state-of-conversational-ai/. Accessed on 29 October 2024.

6 Garner (2024) *Case Study: Generative AI Chatbot Resolves 75% of Customer Interactions*, April 4, https://www.gartner.com/en/documents/5333363. Accessed on 29 October 2024.

7 Bouslov, Gabe (2023) "From zero to GenAI chatbot hero: Step-by-step guide and best practices for building advanced chatbots," *Medium*, September 20, https://medium.com/@gbouslov/from-zero-to-genai-chatbot-hero-29b1f45f6542. Accessed on 29 October 2024.

8 Stryker, Cole (2024) "With generative AI, don't believe the hype (or the anti-hype)," *IBM Blog*, September 3, https://www.ibm.com/blog/with-generative-ai-dont-believe-the-hype-or-the-anti-hype/. Accessed on 29 October 2024.

9 Quach, Katyanna (2020) "AI me to the Moon… Carbon footprint for 'training GPT-3' same as driving to our natural satellite and back," *The Register*, November 4, https://www.theregister.com/2020/11/04/gpt3_carbon_footprint_estimate/. Accessed on 29 October 2024.

10 Li, Pengfei, Yang, Jianyi, Islam, Mohammad A. and Re, Shaolei (2023) "Making AI less 'thirsty': Uncovering and addressing the secret water footprint of AI Models," https://arxiv.org/pdf/2304.03271.pdf. Accessed on 29 October 2024.

11 Villalobos, Pablo, Ho, Anson, Sevilla, Jaime, Besiroglu, Tamay, Heim, Lennart and Hobbhahn, Marius (2024) "Will we run out of data? Limits of LLM scaling based on human-generated data," https://arxiv.org/pdf/2211.04325.pdf. Accessed on 29 October 2024.

12 Srivathsan, Bhargs, Sorel, Marc, Sachdeva, Pankaj, Bhan, Arjita, Batra, Haripreet, Sharma, Raman, Gupta, Rishi and Choudhary, Surbhi (2024) "AI power: Expanding data center capacity to meet growing demand,"

McKinsey & Company, October 29, https://www.mckinsey.com/industries/technology-media-and-telecommunications/our-insights/ai-power-expanding-data-center-capacity-to-meet-growing-demand. Accessed on 29 October 2024.
13 Pezzone, Jimmy (2022) “Nvidia’s Jensen Huang once again claims Moore’s Law is dead,” *Techspot*, https://www.techspot.com/news/96094-nvidia-jensen-huang-once-again-claims-moore-law.html. Accessed on 29 October 2024.
14 Langley, William (2024) “Lenovo sales surge on rising demand for AI infrastructure”, *Financial Times*, August 15, https://www.ft.com/content/f7b95535-f145-47c3-9fe0-f9b9cdfa2c83#post-5ed6e6fe-df2d-40b5-aa1d-3cdb0d84d0b7. Accessed on 29 October 2024.
15 Branwen, Gwern (2020) *The Scaling Hypothesis*, https://gwern.net/scaling-hypothesis. Accessed on 15 November 2024.
16 Bommasani, Rishi and Liang, Percy (2021) “Reflections on foundation models”, *Stanford Institute for Human-Centered Artificial Intelligence*, October 21, https://hai.stanford.edu/news/reflections-foundation-models. Accessed on 30 October 2024.
17 Rebelo, Miguel (2023) “What is Hugging Face?”, May 23, https://zapier.com/blog/hugging-face/. Accessed on 5 November 2024.
18 Datacamp (2023) “What is Hugging Face? The AI community’s open-source oasis”, November 17, https://www.datacamp.com/tutorial/what-is-hugging-face. Accessed on 5 November 2024.
19 https://weaviate.io/. Accessed on 5 November 2024.
20 https://www.langchain.com/. Accessed on 5 November 2024.
21 Cahn, David (2024) “AI’s $600B question,” *Sequoia Capital Blog*, June 20, https://www.sequoiacap.com/article/ais-600b-question/. Accessed on 9 November 2024.
22 This is a straightforward and crude calculation: Assuming GPUs represent half of the total ownership costs, it takes Nvidia’s run-rate revenue forecast and doubles it to account for the full cost of AI data centres, including energy consumption, building infrastructure, and backup generators. See the source reference for the exact figures used.
23 https://pessimistsarchive.org/. Accessed on 5 November 2024.
24 Keynes, Soumaya (Host) (2024) “Rethinking the AI boom, with Daron Acemoğlu”, *The Economics Show with Soumaya Keynes*, https://www.ft.com/content/e865a777-501a-4417-839e-dffd4b5206e7. Accessed on 15 November 2024.
25 Perez, Carlota (2024) “What is AI’s place in history?” *Project Syndicate*, 11 March, https://www.project-syndicate.org/columnist/carlota-perez-1. Accessed on 15 November 2024.

CHAPTER 6

GenAI in Current Business Use

PAUL COULD NOT BELIEVE his ears. After nine months of trying, the team from an international insurance company explained to him how impossible it had been to build a GenAI-powered chatbot that works. So much so that the team has now decided to "suspend indefinitely" its development; this situation certainly contradicts the prevailing impression of companies' adoption of GenAI. If GenAI chatbots can confer so many advantages and be built so easily and quickly, what is stopping the insurance company from following in their footsteps? Is it that complicated to build a chatbot? After all, anyone can build GenAI-driven chatbots in under an hour![1] Returning to the insurance company's predicament, the initial attempt was to make it possible for the robot to sell two health insurance plans. Plan A is designed for retirees seeking post-employment health insurance. Plan B, on the other hand, is for current employees who want to obtain additional health coverage. Simple enough to build a chatbot to sell these two products, you might think. Here is where things get interesting—and potentially problematic. The AI chatbot is impressively knowledgeable and can engage in detailed conversations about both plans. It answers questions smoothly and even makes recommendations.

Everything seems perfect until a customer asks about coverage for alternative medicine. Plan A covers alternative medicine, whereas Plan B does not. This is the point at which our robot gets confused. Despite being programmed to know better, after a long conversation about Plan

DOI: 10.1201/9781003559665-6

B, a potential customer suddenly asks if the said plan covers alternative medicine, and the chatbot says "yes" when, in fact, it does not. This mistake means the chatbot is as reliable as a GPS navigation system that occasionally sends you to the wrong destination, which may be an acceptable exchange on many occasions. However, for a financial services company, this critical error can constitute mis-selling, cost money, and damage the company's reputation.

TRUST NO BOT

In February 2024, Air Canada lost a small claims court case over misleading information provided by its AI-powered chatbot. The verdict has significant implications for companies using AI chatbots for customer service. A passenger was enquiring about bereavement fares after his grandmother's death. Air Canada's website chatbot incorrectly informed him that bereavement fares could be applied retroactively within 90 days of ticket issuance. Acting on this information, the passenger booked his flights and later attempted to claim the bereavement fare discount.

Air Canada rejected his claim, stating that its policy does not allow retroactive bereavement fare applications. The airline offered a $200 flight voucher to resolve the complaint, but he refused it. The case was brought to the court, where the tribunal ruled in favour of the passenger, stating that the airline was liable for negligent misrepresentation. The decision was based on the fact that Air Canada is responsible for information disseminated via its website, including chatbot interactions. The airline was found to have failed in its duty to ensure the accuracy of the information provided by its chatbot. In addition, customers should not be expected to double-check information on the website (and, by extension, the chatbot's answers). This ruling underlines the fact that businesses will be held accountable for the actions of their AI tools, especially in consumer-facing situations.[2]

On the one hand, not a day has gone by without us being reminded how companies have successfully used AI in their operations. A recent study by IDC, commissioned by Microsoft, finds that among its surveyed companies, the adoption of all types of AI has grown steadily from 71% in 2023 to 78% in 2024, while GenAI adoption has increased more rapidly over the same period from 55% to 75%.[3] At the same time, tech giants encourage us to do more. In July 2024, Alphabet's CEO, Sundar Pichai, said, "When we go through a curve like this, the risk of under-investing is dramatically greater than the risk of over-investing for us here."[4]

Nevertheless, *The Economist* has warned us that "AI-boosters will tell you that the technology is transforming the fortunes of this company or that. Don't believe them."[5] Indeed, suppose companies are ready to take on GenAI; why did the tech consulting giant Accenture report in September 2024 that it had booked only $3 billion worth of GenAI client work in the trailing 12 months, against total sales of $81 billion?[6] How come 68% of companies in the US responded in a recent survey by Deloitte to say their organisation has moved less than 30% of their GenAI from proof of concept (POC) to implementation? What could explain that only 8% of companies in 14 countries surveyed say that they have deployed more than half of their GenAI POC?[7] Or why have only 3% of German companies managed to use GenAI on a large scale, while 63% are still stuck at the beginning?[8]

Realising tangible business value from GenAI presents a multifaceted challenge. This chapter systematically examines the primary impediments to the adoption of GenAI and proposes strategic approaches to mitigate these obstacles. Furthermore, it delineates the substantial value proposition that GenAI offers to enterprises. Drawing upon insights derived from our extensive client engagements, this chapter illustrates how GenAI can catalyse transformative outcomes and unlock novel avenues for business growth and innovation. Additionally, it provides critical guidance designed to assist organisations, regardless of size, in avoiding common pitfalls and accelerating their GenAI integration initiatives. Concluding this chapter and Part 1 of this book, we present a synthesis of key takeaways, summarising the foundational concepts discussed herein.

VALUE SOURCES OF GENAI

We will start with the million-dollar question: What is the source of GenAI's benefits? The answer: hard to pinpoint. It seems many companies are no closer to finding the answer either. A survey of 150 executives from European and North American companies making over $1 billion in revenue revealed that 68% of them have not been able to measure the potential impact of GenAI on their business, and only 9% have evaluated the possible gains for specific functions.[9] Put differently, we know there are benefits to be reaped from GenAI, but we do not know how much.

Let us zoom out to the bigger picture for the moment. Logically, what can companies do to create value out of GenAI? The most cited would likely be productivity and, by extension, improvements in operational efficiency. Indeed, 42% of the companies in the Deloitte study declare this to be the most critical benefit achieved to date.[10] Another study reinforces this: GenAI is viewed as an excellent tool for increasing productivity.[11] A boost in productivity as a source of value is perhaps not surprising. In the decade between 2012 and 2022, productivity growth fell below 1% annually, from an average of 2.2% per year in the five years to 2002 and 1.6% per year from 2002 to 2007.[12] (We believe this is likely attributable to the impact of the PC revolution, which started in the mid-1980s and has finally worn off.)

Within the business sphere, the predominant application of GenAI has thus far centred on enhancing productivity. However, the trajectory for transitioning from mere productivity gains to comprehensive, systemic operational enhancement remains considerably less defined. Furthermore, at the current stage of technological maturity, the primary value proposition of GenAI, akin to conventional AI, resides in driving efficiency and cost savings. Conversely, its efficacy as a direct revenue driver remains somewhat elusive. This observation is corroborated by findings from a Deloitte survey, which indicated that only 6% of respondents reported leveraging GenAI to achieve "increased revenue."[13]

THE SHAFT, NOT JUST THE TIP

Building upon the arguments presented in the preceding chapter regarding the critical role of a supportive social and governmental ecosystem for technological proliferation, we contend that a comparable internal ecosystem is indispensable for technological success within an enterprise. Organisations seeking to leverage Artificial Intelligence (AI) effectively must navigate four distinct internal challenges: executive leadership, data infrastructure, existing systems, and workforce capabilities. AI can be conceptualised as the sharpened tip of a spear, capable of penetrating complex challenges and forging new opportunities. However, the ultimate efficacy and destructive power of this AI spearhead are contingent upon the integrity and alignment of its "shaft," which comprises the four aforementioned internal factors. Without a robust and well-integrated organisational "shaft," even the most advanced AI solutions will fail to achieve their intended impact, rendering technological investments largely ineffectual. The subsequent sections will detail each of these critical components sequentially.

Hurdle 1: Management Teams

A primary concern for executive leadership teams centres on risk mitigation. Companies in sectors such as healthcare and financial services, alongside numerous business-to-consumer enterprises, confront substantial legal and regulatory risks due to their fundamental responsibility to safeguard sensitive customer data. Consequently, these organisations must meticulously navigate the continually evolving landscape of privacy and security regulations specifically designed to protect financial and medical information within these highly regulated industries.

Management teams often find themselves in an unenviable position. It has been alleged that chief executives face two opposing fears. On the one hand, they are afraid of being left behind if they adopt too slowly. On the other hand, they fear being embarrassed if they move too rapidly, which could damage their company's reputation.[14] As the CEO of Nexus, Danny found himself becoming more involved in helping senior managers in client firms convince their bosses of AI's merits and offer them the right prescription to manage deployment risk. Their hesitation is understandable. They face a great deal of uncertainty. For instance, many companies are still struggling to measure the benefits of GenAI accurately. The Deloitte survey reveals that over 40% of its respondents have struggled to define and measure the exact impact of their GenAI initiatives.[15] This problem is particularly acute, as many companies have only used qualitative criteria to measure the success of their GenAI POCs. To scale up, quantitative criteria must be developed so that the performance of the GenAI can be evaluated at the enterprise level. Not surprisingly, the lack of quantifiable measures has resulted in only 16% of companies being able to produce regular reports for the CFO regarding the value created by GenAI.[16]

Closely related to this problem is uncertainty over GenAI's return on investment (ROI), as the return is not immediate and may change over time. Nevertheless, companies have reported that with every dollar invested comes an average return of 3.7 times the investment. Equally telling is that just 1% of respondents reported no return on investment (ROI), and only 4% had achieved a break-even point. Indeed, most companies claimed to have at least doubled their initial investment.[17] These numbers suggest that the core inquiry is not whether GenAI can create value but rather how organisations can optimise their strategies and implementation to maximise its benefits. The subsequent discussion will present a suite of tools and conceptual frameworks designed to enhance the likelihood of successful

GenAI (and traditional AI) adoption for management teams. While these recommendations are specifically tailored to the nuances of the financial services sector, companies operating in other industries may nonetheless derive substantial and actionable insights from the principles outlined.

AI Transformation Strategy

A strong digital transformation strategy is critical for modern businesses, akin to a fundamental necessity. It focuses on enhancing current capabilities, anticipating future requirements, and integrating advanced AI technologies to empower organisations. We present a possible AI transformation roadmap, like the one shown in **Figure 6.1**, to highlight the steps in AI development within a firm.

Years 1 and 2 form the foundation of the "getting our acts together" phase, which aims to extract AI-driven efficiency dividends. At this stage, companies streamline their activities by eliminating labour-intensive processes and utilising the previously scattered data that has been brought together. Having laid a solid foundation around years 3 and 4, companies can scale up and augment their capabilities. In five years, companies should be able to expand their AI operations by embedding AI capabilities in both front- and back-end operations, moving away from mere efficiency plays and genuinely transforming the company.

Of course, all journeys must have a starting point. How could a company get off to a quick start with AI? In our client work, we use what we

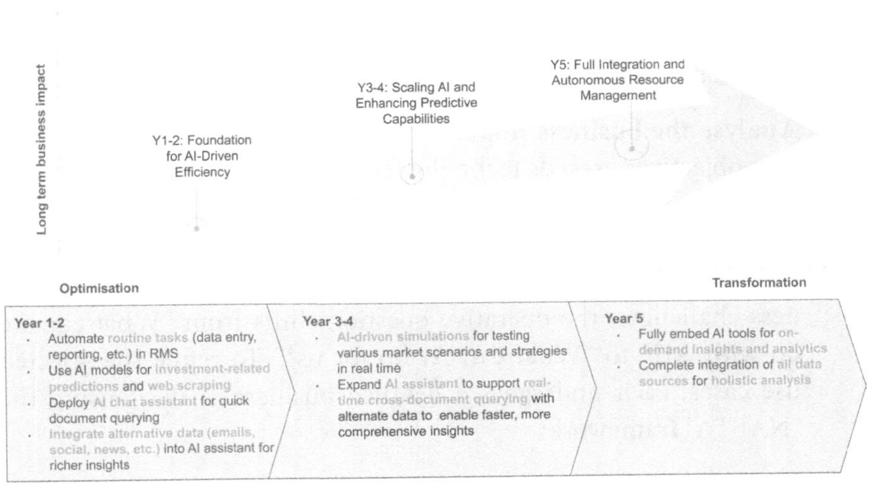

FIGURE 6.1 AI transformation roadmap.

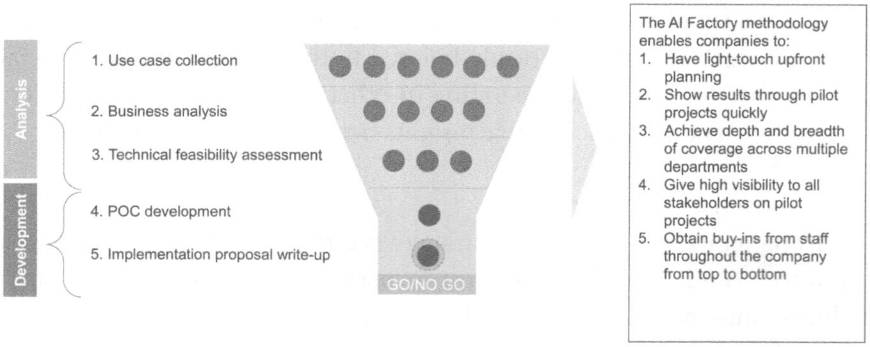

FIGURE 6.2 AI factory.

call the "AI Factory," a methodology that helps organisations identify, prioritise, and execute high-impact AI projects. The AI Factory is shown in **Figure 6.2**, a method that consists of five steps:

1. **Gather use cases ("What is bothering us the most?"):** Identifying viable AI applications begins with a comprehensive organisational assessment to uncover all potential use cases. For example, a UK government agency client's data volume, strategic objectives, and immediate operational demands were analysed to pinpoint areas where AI could alleviate critical pain points. While it is beneficial to compile an exhaustive list of opportunities without initial prejudice, practical constraints, such as our client's identification of over 100 potential applications, necessitate rigorous prioritisation against established criteria before further consideration.

2. **Analyse the business impact ("Will this help?"):** Critically, business objectives precede technological considerations in this process. A company must maintain a laser focus on identifying intrinsic business value rather than being unduly influenced by perceived technological feasibility. Given AI's capacity to address diverse business challenges, the operative question shifts from "What can we do with AI?" to "What can AI do for us?" To refine the selected use cases, each undergoes a detailed business analysis using the "NAFTA" framework:

   Need: Does the use case solve or contribute to a core need of the business?

Alignment: Does the use case align with the company's long-term strategic vision?

Finances: How will the costs and benefits be decided based on the specific use case?

Technological complexity: How complicated is designing and implementing the AI model?

Assessment: What are the model deployment and failure risks, and is there a suitable mitigation strategy?

It is essential to point out that the criteria here do not only consist of direct costs; they must also include indirect ones, such as costs related to workflow changes and people issues.

3. **Assess technical feasibility ("Can we do this?"):** Use cases demonstrating economic potential proceed to a technical evaluation, often through small-scale experiments to showcase AI capabilities. This process involves comparing off-the-shelf, open-source, and bespoke solutions to ensure cost-effective recommendations and provide technological insights without requiring significant upfront investment. The outcome is a recommendations report for each use case, detailing business and technical feasibility, along with preliminary solution designs and architectural suggestions. The most promising use case then advances to a Proof of Concept (POC) phase.
4. **Develop a POC ("Let's give it a shot"):** The Proof of Concept (POC) aims to translate anticipated benefits into initial tangible results. These outcomes are then presented for stakeholder feedback, which informs subsequent pilot improvements in an iterative process. This cycle continues until the business's established success criteria are fully met.
5. **Create an implementation proposal ("Here's how we make it stick"):** The final step involves creating a comprehensive implementation plan informed by POC insights. An initial draft is presented business-wide to gather diverse perspectives that can accelerate delivery and ensure a smooth transition from pilot to full-scale solution. This plan positions the business to make an informed decision on pursuing the AI solution. This "AI Factory" methodology has demonstrably benefited our clients, with large international companies achieving live implementation from ideation in under five months.

Managing the Three Horsemen of AI "Risk-apocalypse"

Media and academia frequently discuss the risks associated with AI, primarily focusing on topics such as hallucinations, ethical concerns, and the automation of injustices. However, risks for company management usually go beyond these. In our experience, many of them will face what can be called the three horsemen of "risk-apocalypse."

Horseman 1: Model traceability: Many AI models operate as "black boxes," providing outputs without transparently revealing their underlying reasoning. This inherent opacity, particularly prevalent in complex systems such as neural networks, impedes the ability to trace decision-making processes and risks the unwitting incorporation of biases from opaque data sources. Several strategies can address these challenges. One approach involves decomposing AI processes into more manageable and auditable components. Another is the establishment of robust decision-tracking systems, which maintain detailed logs of model behaviour. Furthermore, rigorous version control is essential for managing and monitoring changes, facilitating the rapid identification of when and where a model's performance may have degraded with updates or upgrades.

Horseman 2: Quality and accuracy: Data quality deficiencies manifest as hallucinations, bias, and performance degradation. Hallucinations compromise factual accuracy, while bias can lead to discriminatory outcomes by amplifying latent biases in training data. Performance may also diminish as real-world conditions diverge from those in the training data. Solutions include leveraging Retrieval-Augmented Generation (RAG) and vector databases to ground responses in verified information, employing prompt engineering for balanced outputs, and implementing human and multi-AI process validation for critical oversight.

Horseman 3: Data security: Privacy and compliance represent paramount concerns for AI systems, given the pervasive risk of data breaches and their severe ramifications for both organisations and individuals. Security vulnerabilities can expose sensitive training data or enable malicious manipulation through prompt injection and model poisoning. Concurrently, stringent data protection regulations necessitate robust compliance frameworks. Therefore, implementing strong encryption, strict access controls, and effective data masking techniques is indispensable for safeguarding AI systems that process sensitive information.

AI Governance

As organisations rapidly embrace AI, establishing robust governance frameworks has become essential. **Figure 6.3** illustrates a comprehensive model for AI development and deployment within businesses, emphasising clear organisational roles, specialised expert teams, and active management oversight. Crucially, developing enterprise-level policies with clear guidelines and guardrails is vital for managing AI risks. Finally, continuous evaluation through regular monitoring, audits, and performance metrics, coupled with proactive stakeholder management and transparent communication, is indispensable for optimising AI performance and ensuring its responsible use.

Ultimately, effective AI risk management extends beyond mere disaster prevention; it is fundamental to cultivating trust in systems that are increasingly vital for the survival of modern businesses. The objective is not to eliminate all risks, which is as impractical as universal agreement on an office thermostat setting. Instead, the goal is to comprehensively understand, diligently manage, and strategically mitigate risks, thereby enabling the continuous and powerful harnessing of AI's capabilities.

Hurdle 2: Data

The second internal hurdle is data. An uncomfortable truth is uncovered when organisations embark on their AI journey: their data infrastructure is not ready or in good shape. Companies frequently face a constellation

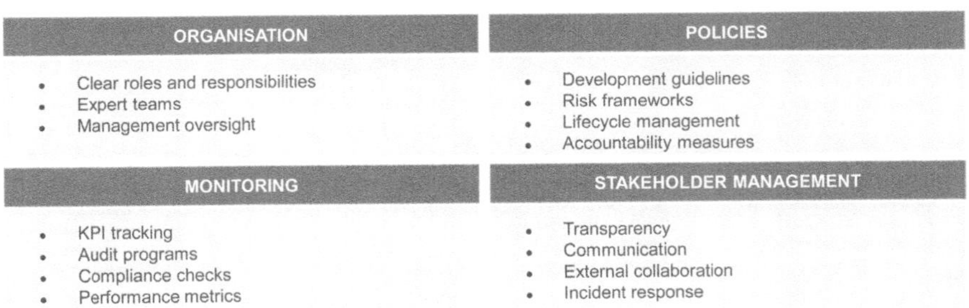

FIGURE 6.3 A comprehensive model for AI development and deployment within businesses.

of challenges, ranging from data silos and unstructured data to a lack of proper means to utilise structured data effectively.

Data Framework

For many organisations, this situation presents a strategic opportunity to holistically organise data, transforming it into a launchpad for future AI initiatives. The initial step requires establishing a robust data framework. In our assessment, such a framework rests upon four foundational pillars, as illustrated in **Figure 6.4**: foundation, execution, governance, and collaboration. The foundation pillar involves setting clear business objectives and formulating a comprehensive data strategy. The execution pillar focuses on architecture, technology selection, and operational procedures. The final pillar is collaboration; though seemingly tangential to data, it is arguably the most critical for long-term success. Even the most elegantly designed AI solutions are likely to falter if not complemented by effective human involvement.

Data Democratisation

For effective AI development, data must be readily accessible, not siloed or fragmented across disparate systems. Many businesses still contend with disorganised data in various formats, which significantly impedes AI training efforts. Such fragmented and unstructured data exacerbates the risk of AI hallucinations and errors during model development.[18] Terence

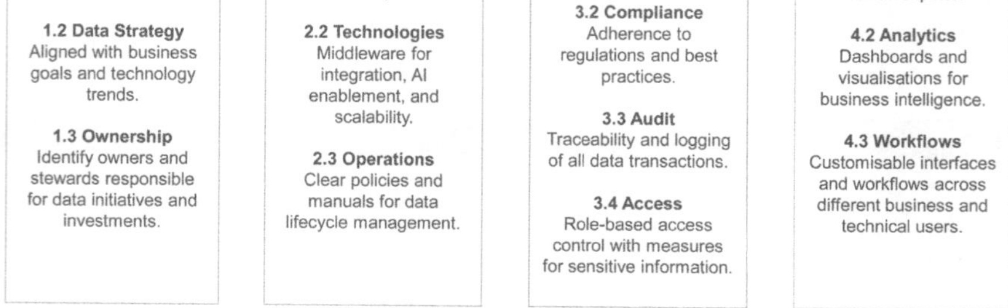

FIGURE 6.4 A data framework.

heard the middle management team of a large UK company complain that they could have easily and rapidly developed innovative products had they been able to consolidate the data sitting idly in different business functions. Organisations will increasingly access a broader range of data, including email records, meeting notes, global news, and social media, thereby unlocking new possibilities. The imperative is to dismantle existing data silos. Ultimately, sophisticated AI platforms will transform data access into a digital buffet, enabling rapid and effortless consumption of insights.

Data Traceability: The Missing Link in Enterprise AI Success

In today's rapidly evolving business landscape, many organisations exhibit an outdated mindset when implementing artificial intelligence, treating it akin to traditional software with clear, predictable input-output patterns. While familiar, this approach is inadequate for the complexities of modern AI systems. While conventional software development allows for straightforward testing and validation, with developers confidently asserting, "We know what data went in and what results should come out," GenAI introduces new complexities and risks that demand a fundamentally different framework.

THE COST OF AI UNCERTAINTY

The emergence of GenAI tools has introduced a critical challenge: hallucinations. These instances occur when AI systems generate factually incorrect, irrelevant, or entirely fabricated responses. Even high-performing AI systems boasting 90% accuracy—a benchmark many organisations struggle to achieve—harbour a concerning 10% chance of producing erroneous results. This margin of error extends beyond mere technical inconvenience; it represents a substantial business risk, particularly in sectors where output accuracy is crucial, such as the financial services industry.

The financial implications of this uncertainty are significant. A 10% error rate could translate into millions lost through lawsuits, regulatory penalties, and client compensation. Unlike traditional algorithmic systems, where errors follow predictable patterns and can be systematically addressed, GenAI's mistakes can be arbitrary and complex, if at all possible, to predict or trace. This unpredictability has created organisational paralysis, preventing many firms from fully leveraging AI's transformative potential. Indeed, traditional software testing and implementation methods are ill-suited for AI, leaving firms unsure of how to test and validate accuracy effectively. This uncertainty creates adoption challenges and leads to broader issues, such as reduced reliability, diminished confidence, audit difficulties, and complications with future regulatory compliance.

DATA TRACEABILITY: THE STRATEGIC SOLUTION

Data traceability emerges as a transformative solution, enabling companies to map AI outputs back to their source inputs. This capability bridges the critical gap between AI's potential and organisations' need for reliability, transforming how companies validate and trust AI outputs through several key mechanisms:

Comprehensive accountability: Organisations can trace specific outputs to their input data, establishing comprehensive audit trails for AI decision-making. This capability enables teams to pinpoint error sources precisely, whether due to data quality issues, algorithmic bias, or interpretation errors, and implement targeted preventive measures. Understanding the root cause of mistakes facilitates continuous improvement and refinement of AI systems.

Proactive hallucination prevention: Real-time verification of outputs against source materials reduces the risk of unreliable results. This capability allows organisations to quickly identify and correct error patterns, maintaining system reliability while building confidence in AI-generated outputs. This proactive quality control transforms AI from a potential liability into a trusted business tool.

Building confidence in AI adoption: By establishing clear connections between AI models, development processes, and underlying data, companies can confidently integrate AI into existing validation frameworks. This process transforms AI deployment from a venture into an uncertain endeavour into a measured advancement, enabling innovation while maintaining appropriate risk controls. The transparency afforded by data traceability allows companies to demonstrate responsible AI use to stakeholders, regulators, and customers.

Enhanced quality assurance: AI significantly enhances code coverage testing, which measures the proportion of code executed during automated tests. Unlike traditional methods, AI comprehends the context of business functions, enabling it to prioritise critical areas like payment processing or data security. This intelligent approach focuses testing on scenarios most relevant to business operations, leading to improved bug detection with reduced effort. For example, AI would extensively test an e-commerce system's checkout process over its "About Us" page, ensuring more effective and targeted testing.

The lesson for organisations is clear: data traceability is an indispensable infrastructure for effective AI leverage. Technology vendors must embed traceability into their AI offerings, merging accuracy with transparency to ensure accountability and transparency. Organisations can no longer tolerate AI solutions prioritising accuracy at the expense of transparency, which limits insight into decision-making processes. We have reached a technological state where high precision can be integrated with unparalleled openness, even in GenAI systems. By combining accuracy with traceability, organisations achieve optimal results and the insights necessary for complete understanding and trust. Only this dynamic duo enables scalable and reliable enterprise-wide AI adoption.

Organisations embracing data traceability early will be better positioned in the evolving AI landscape. Approaching current AI systems with a linear, transparent software development mentality will create significant business challenges; this lack of transparency hinders trust and exposes companies to unforeseen risks in an increasingly regulated environment. Data traceability is a critical foundation for responsible AI development and deployment. For companies seeking to harness AI's transformative power while maintaining control and accountability, robust traceability is no longer merely a best practice but an absolute necessity for success in the AI-driven future. As AI integrates more deeply into business processes, tracing and validating AI-driven decisions will become increasingly crucial for achieving a competitive advantage and long-term success.

Hurdle 3: IT Systems

The antiquated nature of many IT systems, often referred to as technical debt, poses significant challenges for AI implementation and exacerbates security vulnerabilities. While discussions surrounding AI frequently emphasise algorithms and use cases, the crucial reality is that successful

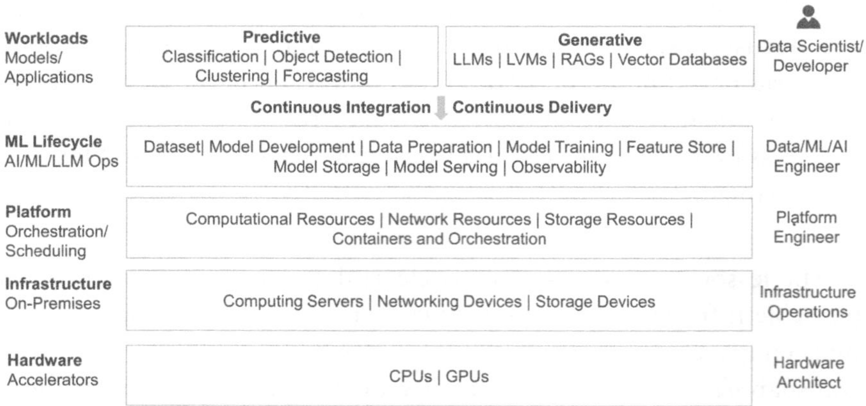

FIGURE 6.5 An IT tech sandwich.

AI deployment fundamentally depends on robust technical infrastructure. Beyond age, IT stacks are increasingly burdened with additional components, augmenting system size and management complexity, thereby introducing more decision-making considerations. As a Head of IT at a major UK company recently conveyed to Terence, cloud service providers actively strive to maximise switching costs, effectively locking in enterprise users. Consequently, she must continually seek alternatives and make decisions that prevent over-reliance on a single cloud vendor, vastly complicating IT management.

Indeed, the IT stack is sometimes referred to as an "IT tech sandwich" due to the continuous addition of layers. As **Figure 6.5** illustrates, integrating AI into the IT system necessitates additional layers and substantial resources, making these "sandwiches" increasingly deluxe and supreme. This more capable, yet undeniably more complex, AI-supported IT system demands diverse IT expertise, ranging from data scientists to hardware architects. Regardless of the IT stack's magnitude, three overarching concerns persist: firstly, security, which is vital to a company's data and reputation; secondly, disaster recovery, necessitating regular backups and contingency plans; and thirdly, scalability, requiring a flexible scaling plan to augment the existing system for new demands and requirements seamlessly.

Migration and Conversation

Effective AI implementation critically depends on the successful completion of migration and conversion phases, ensuring that AI technology functions as intended and delivers the expected benefits. Migration involves transferring data or software between systems, while conversion transforms old IT systems. Legacy code and undocumented systems often complicate these processes, resulting in delays, increased costs, and potential project failures. Poorly managed migration and conversion can significantly diminish ROI, turning promising AI initiatives into costly endeavours.

Think strategically: Successful AI integration transcends mere technical implementation, demanding a strategic approach that aligns technology with broader business objectives. This approach necessitates close collaboration among strategy, business, and finance teams. For instance, finance must develop a comprehensive plan that anticipates potential delays and cost adjustments, thereby preventing budget overruns—a common cause of failed technology implementations.

Prepare for the unknowns: Even experienced IT executives cannot foresee every challenge in technological transformation. Unpredictable "unknown unknowns" will inevitably emerge, requiring a flexible and resilient environment. Building a corporate culture that embraces transparency and open communication allows unexpected obstacles to become opportunities for innovation. Successful AI implementation focuses not on eliminating all risks but on establishing a robust framework that can rapidly adapt and respond to challenges, thereby mitigating costly delays or project failures.

A small step can lead to substantial progress: The "divide and conquer" strategy proves highly effective in AI implementation. Rather than an all-encompassing transformation, focusing on small, manageable deliverables allows end-users to gradually adapt to new workflows, fostering confidence and increasing acceptance. This incremental approach significantly lowers overall project risk by generating momentum through consistent small wins. Each success reduces the likelihood of failure and presents valuable opportunities for ongoing improvement.

Stop the sprawl: In their pursuit of advanced technology, many companies accumulate an excessive number of external providers, leading to "tech sprawl" and complex middleware. This situation complicates management and drains resources. The solution lies in strategic consolidation: reducing vendor relationships and partnering with technology providers who understand AI migration. This approach streamlines the technological environment, allowing organisations to focus resources on integrating AI to drive business value.

Hurdle 4: Talents

Staff development is not optional in the AI era. The battle for AI talent has been intensifying over the past years. The talent challenge in AI continues to strengthen. Companies face a growing shortage of AI-proficient professionals, with AI-related job postings in the US increasing by 122% in 2024, representing an 18% growth from the year before. GenAI arguably drives this surge as employers seek expertise in ChatGPT, prompt engineering, and large language models (LLMs).[19] Nevertheless, the demand for talent is not confined to technical roles. Organisations increasingly value AI literacy across all functions. A telling example: Sales representatives with AI skills can command a $45,000 annual premium over their non-AI-savvy peers.[20]

It is no wonder that "lack of skilled workers" was the most frequently given response when asked what challenges companies have experienced or expect when implementing AI technology in their companies in IDC's survey.[21] This situation is in line with the findings in the Deloitte study, which found that only 20% of companies are prepared for this issue, lower than other problems related to risk and governance (23%), strategy (37%), data management (41%), and technology infrastructure (45%).[22]

GenAI is poised to accelerate workplace productivity and significantly revamp operating models. Consequently, companies will face increasing pressure to rapidly assess their talent and skill requirements, implement diverse strategies to bridge skill gaps and invest in both upskilling and reskilling initiatives. However, relying solely on hiring will be insufficient to close the talent deficit. Organisations must adopt a novel approach to equip their existing workforce better. Becoming an AI-enabled enterprise necessitates prioritising the development of the next-generation workforce and the human element of GenAI. To achieve this, businesses should consider three key dimensions: overcoming resistance, human-in-the-loop (HITL) integration, and robust oversight.

Overcoming Resistance

A review of the literature on AI integration reveals a consensus among consultants, technologists, and academics regarding the complexities of technological adoption. These insights converge on two primary mechanisms for mitigating organisational resistance: bolstering employee motivation and fostering usage inertia. Cultivating genuine employee motivation is paramount. As Danny observed in numerous client engagements, from global banks to traditional industries, organisational change is inherently challenging; entities often cling to established routines, leading staff to resist unfamiliar patterns.

At the same time, Danny has also observed that deep down, individuals intrinsically desire growth and meaning, even as responsibilities tether them to conventional career paths. This dynamic is particularly evident in the transition to AI-enabled operations, which necessitates a holistic transformation of people, processes, systems, and mindsets. Technology merely facilitates executive vision; fundamental change demands dedicated effort, including overcoming resistance, educating personnel, executing integration plans, and ensuring staff proficiency with new technologies.

Our extensive client work reveals a proven AI adoption strategy: comprehensive education and training across three key groups. Initially, we provide workshops for senior executives to foster a strategic understanding of AI, demonstrating its potential to drive innovation, enhance decision-making, and support sustainable growth. Subsequently, we collaborate closely with IT teams, facilitating deep knowledge transfer and ongoing support, transforming them into strategic enablers of AI transformation. Finally, we deliver targeted training to end-users, building practical skills and confidence. Alternatively, in some engagements, training is offered to executive teams and end-users, with workshops for managers and policy owners who are responsible for centralised configurations and frameworks, enabling proper oversight of novel technologies. These efforts empower every employee to effectively utilise new AI solutions, translating technological potential into real-world performance. Why acquire state-of-the-art AI systems without providing staff with the necessary operational training?[23]

The key here is not just improving employees' technical skills—it is about fostering an environment where they willingly embrace technology to boost performance. Financial incentives alone, such as the $45,000 premium mentioned earlier, are unlikely to be enough to sustain motivation. Research shows that willpower and self-discipline act like muscles: they can become fatigued.[24] Willpower also depletes much faster when workers feel they are following orders without agency.[25] A 2010 study at an Ohio manufacturing plant demonstrated this effect. When assembly-line workers were allowed to make small decisions, such as designing their uniforms and managing shift schedules, productivity increased by 20% within two months. Moreover, workers took shorter breaks, made fewer mistakes, and demonstrated greater self-discipline without altering their processes or pay.[26] For companies aiming to become AI-powered, employee training and education must go beyond technical skills; they must be matched by rethinking new processes and workflows that incorporate choice.

Training, combined with increased motivation and choice, can foster lasting habits and drive the adoption of tools. Here is a telling example that a consultant shared with Terence. An optional Microsoft Copilot course was offered to some of its 100 employees at a publishing company. By the end of the training, the 30 participants who completed it had continued to use Copilot daily, even though the company primarily relies on Google Workspace—and not Microsoft 365—for business and collaboration. This example yields three key insights. Firstly, not all individuals will embrace new technology; some workers will inevitably resist or remain indifferent to technological changes. Secondly, training extends beyond mere upskilling: practical instruction enhances technical skills and cultivates interest, boosting motivation and fostering autonomy. Engaged employees are more likely to perceive the value of new tools and technologies. Thirdly, training generates usage momentum. Even when tools like Microsoft Copilot and Google Workspace are not perfectly integrated, enthusiastic employees will persist in utilising them. This phenomenon highlights the crucial role of education in driving the adoption of technology.

Companies should take advantage of the fact that many of their staff have already transformed into secret cyborgs, using GenAI at work even as their employers dawdle. As of August 2024, 39% of US adults were found to be using GenAI. Over 24% of workers reported using it at least once a week, and nearly one in nine used it daily.[27] In contrast, just under 6% of US companies use GenAI for their businesses.[28] It is only a matter of time before more workers take up GenAI. When motivated workers choose to use AI technology with interest, companies may also leverage this trend.

Human in the Loop

"Shock therapy" is unhelpful for digital transformation. As observed in client banks where routines are sacrosanct, disruption is perceived as a threat. However, by gradually introducing tools aligned with existing mindsets, organisations can subtly nudge towards innovation. The objective is to integrate solutions with current practices, creating incremental changes that reshape the environment over time.

This process contradicts the erroneous belief that more powerful AI models inherently lead to better business offerings. The true power of AI derives not from model prowess or technology but from the correct business setup and infrastructure to optimally utilise model output. By introducing humans into the loop at every stage, the transformation becomes a journey of co-creation, where technology and people reciprocally adapt to each other. HITL, following the definition of Stanford University's Human-Centred Artificial Intelligence, refers to the approach that reframes an automation problem as a human-computer interaction design problem. It broadens the question of "how do we build a smarter system?" to "how do we incorporate useful, meaningful human interaction into the system?"[29] The benefits of HITL are twofold: it lowers barriers to change and strengthens the ability to oversee and improve algorithm performance.

For example, for the expert compliance team of one of our clients, a global bank, the days of "eyeballing" the details on PDF documents submitted by customers, manually performing checks, and entering data into the database are now behind us. The team now supervises the algorithms we have designed and built to take over these manual tasks. By providing them with the necessary training and making adjustments to the processes, the compliance staff have fully embraced the AI system, which has now elevated all of them to machine supervisors. This role change also involves the team reviewing and correcting algorithm outputs, resulting in improved model accuracy and creating a more effective and efficient sales quality checking operation. Additional advantages of the HITL structure include mitigation of model bias risk and enhancing sustainability and scalability.

Scaling up AI within a company effectively means getting more staff to use the AI system. We are building a platform for the sustainable finance team worldwide on behalf of another client. The team itself plays a crucial role in the cascading user expansion strategy. Starting with the team in EMEA as the initial user group, this will enable them to operate an AI-driven platform, thereby improving data collection and analytical capabilities. Subsequent user groups from the Americas will be able to utilise the new features offered on the AI platform to collect more data and perform analyses, which further enrich the platform's content and utility.

The APAC team will join the fray next, adding their data and analyses. This approach fosters a collaborative and iterative platform development process, where each new region contributes to and benefits from the accumulated knowledge and insights. Building a comprehensive, AI-driven global sustainable finance framework is only possible through human-machine collaboration.

HITL is not an end in itself but a proven mechanism for navigating inevitable AI-driven change. This transformation rarely concerns technology alone; it involves untangling a complex web of interdependencies. People desire progress while also seeking stability. Technology offers viable solutions only if it aligns with an organisation's social, cultural, and economic realities. Ultimately, innovation is defined not merely by available tools but by how they are combined with existing constraints and opportunities.

ILLUSTRATION: GENAI SOLUTIONS

Leveraging GenAI often requires it to be combined with traditional AI. As shown in **Figure 6.6**, a repeat of Figure 3.2, technologies must be effectively integrated into business operations, ensuring that data, IT, and talent all work together as seamlessly as possible. We believe that only by doing this can new GenAI-driven value propositions be found. Here, we present two such possibilities based on our work with clients.

One possibility is extracting and analysing data from bond prospectuses. Navigating complex bond prospectuses presents a significant challenge for asset managers. The sheer volume of information, combined with strict deadlines, often impedes their ability to assess legal and financial risks accurately and compromises analytical thoroughness. AI algorithms

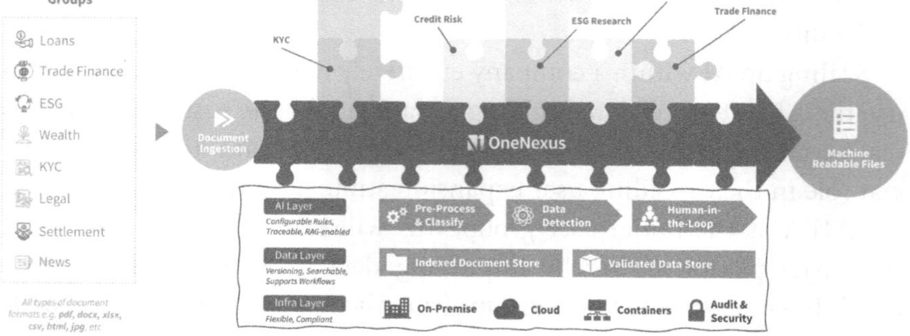

FIGURE 6.6 The "OneNexus" platform.

can address this by automating and streamlining information processing, such as populating analytical models. We are helping a well-known global asset management company establish a combined traditional and GenAI solution to extract vast amounts of unstructured data from prospectuses and use it to perform the required analyses. The output would then be presented on user-friendly dashboards, making it easier and faster for asset managers to identify economic opportunities and associated risks.

Another possibility is research management. Research is an indispensable part of any investment company. Better research directly translates into a better understanding of risks and returns. Unfortunately, there are two significant challenges. Firstly, identifying the necessary data, extracting and converting it into structured data, and formatting it correctly to produce analyses is exceptionally labour-intensive and time-consuming. Secondly, collected data and existing analyses must be continually updated. Acting on outdated information or failing to respond sufficiently rapidly to sudden changes can be costly financially.

These data problems are particularly acute for investment companies that cover environmental, social, and governance (ESG), a set of standards by which a company's operations, as well as its impact on the environment and society, are evaluated. These criteria have gained prominence among investors and stakeholders prioritising sustainable and ethical business practices.[30] Investment companies need to be aware of any changes to the ESG status of the companies in their portfolios, as a negative change can significantly reduce the value of an investee. To help mitigate this problem for an international institutional client, we have developed a system that utilises both traditional and GenAI approaches to assist with their research.

GenAI, when combined with web scraping, can monitor and analyse news published worldwide. Current AI technology can recognise trends, discern abnormal events, and detect sentiment in multiple languages (at Nexus, it is English and Chinese), all of which enable investment companies to react and respond to emerging issues promptly. GenAI can also be integrated into the dashboard for ESG research and scoring. This process entails once again combining both traditional and GenAI systems for vast data integration, cleansing, standardisation, and scoring. Automating and analysing data that complies with the required ESG rules (different companies have different ones), updating scores in real-time, and tracking progress make reliable ESG information and metrics available to investment managers. In turn, these managers will be able to continuously

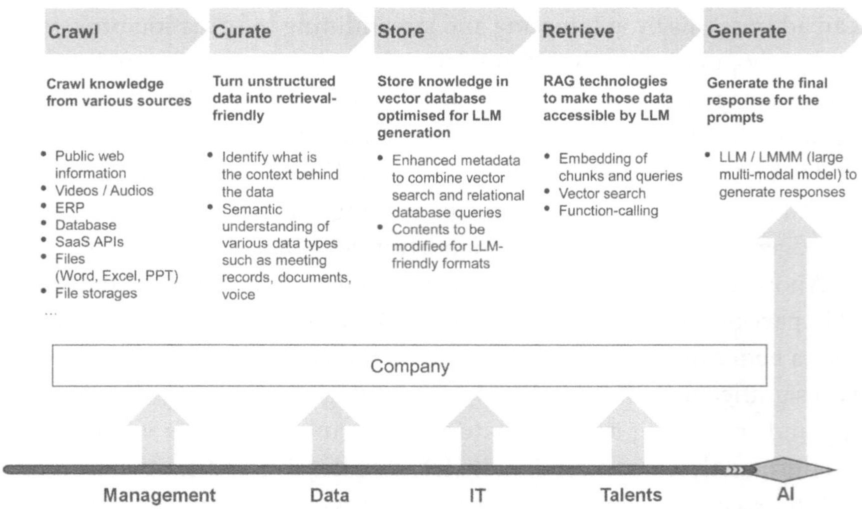

FIGURE 6.7 An overview of the chain of actions and components of GenAI business deployment.

monitor companies' ESG status. Additionally, with just a click, they can generate reports that quickly compile all the necessary content and present it in the required structures and formats. As a result, investment managers will merely have to focus on editing and finalising the machine-produced drafts before publishing.

These experiences offer a salient lesson for the application of GenAI in business: while a powerful tool for user interaction, the technology's efficacy is contingent upon proper and robust support. **Figure 6.7** presents an overview of the chain of actions and components—both business and technical—that must be in place for GenAI to generate the proper responses for end users.

MACHINES ARE NOT HUMANS, AFTER ALL

Management teams, data, systems, and talents are critical factors in how businesses can adopt GenAI. Nevertheless, none of these explains the insurance company's predicament described at the start of this chapter. This situation baffled Paul, who set himself to trace the root cause. Ultimately, he managed to get to the bottom of it: how GenAI works (and does not work). The advent of ChatGPT represents a watershed moment in technological innovation. However, beneath the surface of this GenAI marvel lies a complex landscape of challenges.

At the core of the problem lies a fundamental misconception regarding LLMs. While capable of generating human-like text, answering complex questions, and engaging in seemingly intelligent conversations, these models function as "talking" rather than "thinking" systems. This distinction necessitates the use of RAG and vector databases to perform the rigorous information retrieval and contextual processing required for accurate and grounded responses.

This brings us back to our insurance company. It appears that a single, comprehensive text corpus designed to cover multiple insurance plans inevitably leads to contextual confusion. GenAI struggles to think clearly and inadvertently mixes features from different plans. Unfortunately, the company's challenges do not end there. It was aiming to offer a flash sale on just one of the two plans. However, with the current setup of the GenAI-driven chatbot, it kept mistakenly applying this discount to the other plan. This demonstrates that even if they manage to set everything up correctly, the company would still face complications and issues when making future changes to the chatbot. This situation is not a technical glitch but a fundamental structural limitation of current GenAI technologies. They cannot establish clear boundaries between different informational contexts, rendering them unreliable for complex, multifaceted business interactions.

This experience also highlighted another issue: the design team must possess comprehensive information about the products offered and consider all potential eventualities and ramifications. For instance, if we aim to create a chatbot that sells travel and pet insurance, we need not only complete information on both products but also answers to all the potential questions that customers may ask, such as how the two policies can operate concurrently when travelling with a dog. Compounding these issues is the fact that much of the critical knowledge required for chatbot design, particularly regarding insurance products, is often tacit—unwritten, experiential understanding that seasoned professionals develop over time. Experienced human agents instinctively recognise context-specific risks that are not explicitly programmed. For example, when a customer books a trip to Japan during cherry blossom season, a human agent immediately recognises that this timing creates unique vulnerabilities (overbooked accommodations, rural medical facility limitations, and weather-dependent viewing conditions) and recommends specific coverage upgrades, such as "Cancel for Any Reason." This nuanced risk assessment derives from patterns observed across hundreds of similar cases—experiential knowledge that cannot be easily codified into chatbot algorithms.

These factors have collectively posed challenges to the production of genuinely effective GenAI-powered solutions. Unlike human agents, who adapt and gain experience over time, chatbots can only replicate such nuanced behaviours if they are explicitly coded. Ultimately, these are not merely technical challenges but fundamental business issues. While individuals can now delegate complex tasks to AI systems in ways previously unimaginable, what works effectively for an individual user does not automatically scale or prove effective for an entire business.

THE BLIND SPOT OF AI ADOPTION

ChatGPT's advent created a cultural sensation, with media and tech CEOs heralding the demise of human labour as machines mimicked human communication and thought. Subsequently, new GenAI products flood the market daily, with LLM creators continually releasing faster, cheaper, and more powerful models. Despite this progress, AI's benefits flow disproportionately to resource-rich entities. Microsoft and Google have integrated GenAI into their office suites, creating tireless assistants that automate tasks such as making presentations and drafting emails. While impressive, these are general solutions optimised for the masses, not the specific problems confronting small- and medium-sized enterprises (SMEs). A bakery requires automated inventory orders when supplies run low, not enhanced spreadsheets. A dental clinic needs patient follow-up tracking, not AI-generated emails.

Herein lies a paradox: AI is simultaneously ubiquitous and elusive—embedded in everyday applications yet inaccessible to those who need it most. The barrier is structural: building custom AI solutions demands specialised business and technical expertise. While Fortune 500 companies can afford this, for family-owned restaurants or regional logistics firms, this structural problem is often insurmountable.

Figure 6.8 shows a recent survey that found larger firms with 100 or more employees have an AI usage rate higher than that of any other size. This fact is perhaps unsurprising. What is interesting, however, is that firms with fewer than five staff also use more AI, which is likely because these four-person bands are more agile and nimble in adopting some AI (especially the readily accessible GenAI). In contrast, SMEs of different sizes may face more barriers to AI adoption, such as limited budgets, less technical expertise, a lack of scale to adopt expensive AI solutions, and underdeveloped IT systems. A recent global survey of 79,000 SMEs found that only one in ten uses AI regularly. The reason is that companies fear

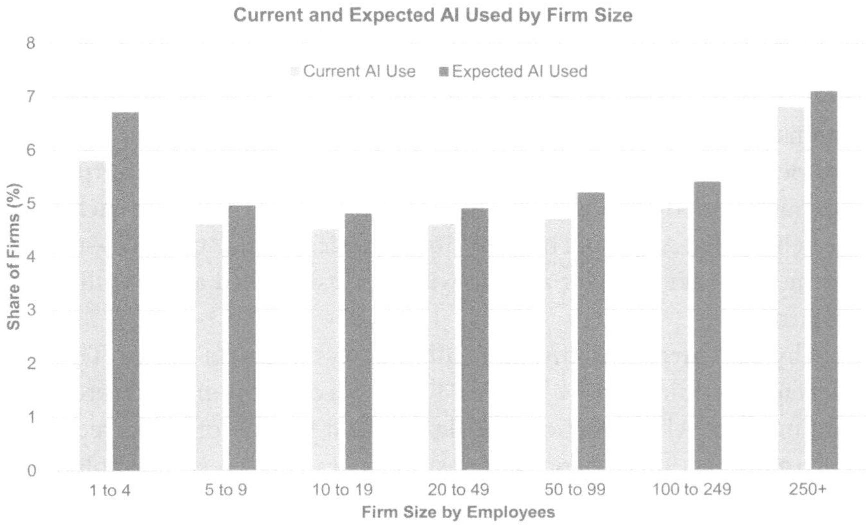

FIGURE 6.8 Current and expected AI use by firm size.

the unknown when it comes to AI, which results from a lack of knowledge and confidence about implementing AI effectively, safely, and compliantly.[31] Put differently, the barrier is not scepticism—it is accessibility.

AI SOLUTIONS FOR SMALL- AND MEDIUM-SIZED ENTERPRISES

The "U-shaped" AI uptake phenomenon, depicted in the figure, highlights a critical gap: the underutilisation of AI by SMEs. While discussions on "democratising" AI often point to the theoretical accessibility provided by LLMs from entities like OpenAI, practical usability remains distinct from theoretical access. What is urgently needed is AI that SMEs can genuinely leverage—tools that are affordable, simple to implement, and designed to enhance existing workflows without demanding specialised machine learning expertise or extensive infrastructure. Consequently, a familiar pattern emerges: larger entities gain greater advantages, faster movers accelerate further, and others lag. True AI democratisation extends beyond mere availability; it mandates genuine usability for those who most require it.

For the past several years, Paul has helped SMEs navigate the AI gold rush, witnessing firsthand the chasm between promise and practice. His clients (like Mabel mentioned in the sidebar) keep asking for AI solutions, but many existing solutions are woefully unsuitable for businesses of their size. Nevertheless, Paul observes that what they need is a way to bring their workflow chaos under control. This is where companies like *Graiphene* come in, putting the power of AI into the hands of SMEs, enabling them to automate their most painful business processes with little or no technical knowledge. The purpose is not to create yet another general-purpose AI tool but to empower businesses to solve the unique challenges each faces. We believe that AI should be accessible, practical, and actionable—not just for the tech-savvy but for anyone with a pressing need and a willingness to learn.

Why can current GenAI not fully address business needs? The chat interface, popularised by ChatGPT, has become the public's predominant mode of AI interaction. While excellent for one-off tasks requiring human interaction and correction, such as drafting a resume or planning a trip, it is designed to solve the "single-task-at-hand" problem, which makes it ill-suited for automated, workflow-based tasks—a significant limitation that requires constant human intervention. SMEs require a platform that accommodates various business considerations, including scalability, reliability, redundancy, expandability, interoperability, and security.

As a one-woman operation, she provides tax reporting services to small businesses, ranging from local restaurants to Amazon vendors. With decades of experience and trusty accounting software, she can file all sixty of her clients' taxes in under a month.

This is, of course, provided all the clients' data are entered into the software.

"I am not afraid of the Tax code, but I'm afraid of Ctrl-C/Ctrl-V," said Mabel. Quickly locating, finding and pinpointing the exact information in bank statements, invoices and receipts and inputting them into the accounting software takes up 80% of her team's time. Here is the problem: she has no alternative but to hire part-time help to do the labour-intensive work. "This work is essential. Yet, it is extremely tedious and prone to error. I'm sure AI can fly through this work, but we don't know how to make that happen."

Stories like Mabel's underscored a broader truth: while AI is accessible to large companies, as mentioned in Chapter 2, there remains a blind spot in the market. While researchers focused on scaling laws and the performance of LLMs, SMEs needed practical tools—AI that could seamlessly integrate into existing workflows, requiring no PhD to set up and maintain. This is where Graiphene comes in.

HOW GRAIPHENE WORKS

The goal of Graiphene is simple: plug-and-play workflow automation. The philosophy behind this SME AI solution echoes the industrialists of the 1920s, who transformed factories into assembly lines. Every business is arguably a series of processes—some managed by humans, others by machines. Therefore, the key to extending AI benefits to SMEs is to help them map and automate these processes. Hence, a logical approach is to make workflows programmable. By translating business processes into visual diagrams—a canvas of nodes and connections—users can implement AI in specific steps, as illustrated in **Figure 6.9**. A node could be a chatbot managing customer complaints, a database logging orders, or a conditional alert ("If prawn stock is less than 20%, notify the manager"). The system handles the rest, enabling the seamless integration of AI and traditional automation. The power of Graiphene rests on leveraging humans' cognitive tendencies by presenting AI interaction models in an immediately understandable format.

Fundamentally, Graiphene has developed an AI system that functions like a flow chart, breaking down complex interactions into discrete, manageable pathways. To address the challenges mentioned earlier faced by the insurance company, Graiphene can create separate, isolated pathways for different insurance plans. In this way, the alternative medicine coverage and the flash discount introduced in one product or pathway cannot be applied to another product or pathway. Breaking down a process also has the additional benefit of adding flexibility. The user can swiftly and

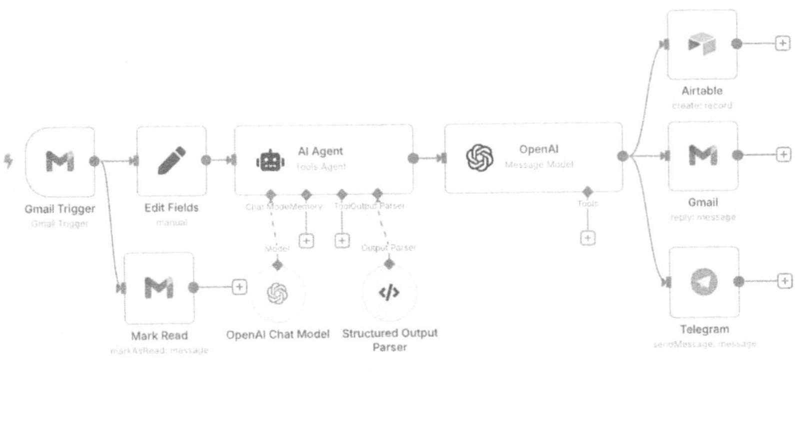

FIGURE 6.9 A screenshot of Graiphene's user interface.

efficiently introduce new features or modify existing ones without risking system-wide disruptions.

So far, the focus is on assisting SMEs in structuring and enhancing their workflows with AI. However, it is equally important to consider the ease of system setup. After signing up, Graiphene initiates a conversation with the user to understand their business and identify key pain points. Indeed, even the drag-and-drop interface depicted in **Figure 6.9** may be too intimidating for the average user. Users seek a solution, not merely an "easier way to programme."

To minimise the learning curve as much as possible, Graiphene developed a specialised LLM, trained on various business scenarios, common challenges faced by SMEs, best-practice solutions, trade-offs, and case studies, to facilitate dialogue. Having needed to manage everything themselves, SME owners must, rightly so, dedicate most of their time to running their businesses. As a result, they do not have the luxury of time or knowledge to systematically streamline and automate their operations. To help with this, the LLM acts as a business specialist, interviewing the user and guiding the process to create an optimised and automated workflow (see sidebar for a typical conversation).

While there are competitors to Graiphene in the market, including n8n, Make, and Zapier, Graiphene distinguishes itself by not assuming or requiring that users are competent programmers. Although these other products may provide excellent bridges for traditional programmers to integrate AI features into their work, they can be utterly demoralising for ordinary users. Consequently, Graiphene considers SME business users as "first-class citizens." When a user signs up, they are asked a few questions about their business and the problem they are attempting to solve, and all necessary information is generated for them. The user can, of course, fine-tune it subsequently.

Figure 6.10 illustrates the onboarding process for creating a custom workflow. The goal is to develop an appropriate workflow for this specific user through a straightforward conversation. Consequently, the chatbot is fine-tuned to elicit the customer's needs in an easy-to-follow dialogue. The experience is crafted to instil a sense of being in the hands of an expert for the user.

The result of the conversation is a workflow that resembles **Figure 6.11**. A casual glance reveals a workflow triggered by receiving an email, followed by some logic, with the answers recorded in a Google Sheet at the end. A knowledgeable user can easily create this from scratch, but doing

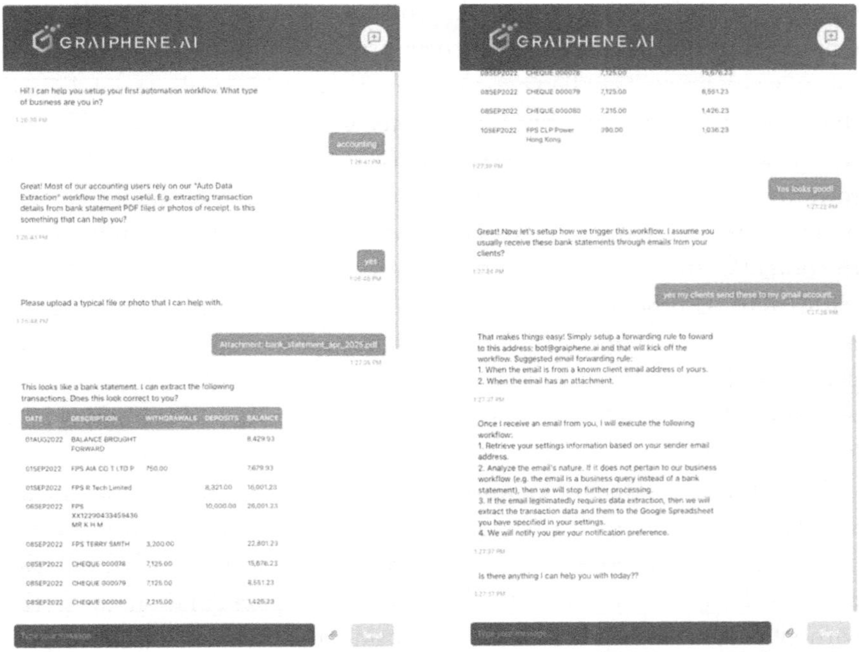

FIGURE 6.10 An example of the conversation between Graiphene and a user.

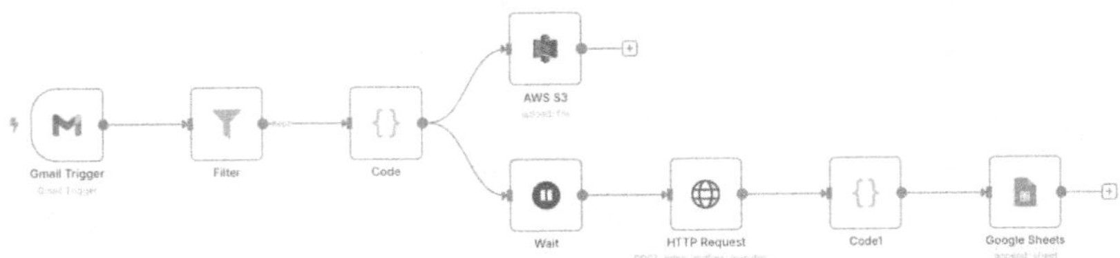

FIGURE 6.11 The workflow generated from the conversation.

so requires a significant amount of technical knowledge. In contrast, Graiphene's approach to having a dedicated "business expert chatbot" will greatly simplify the process for busy SME owners and managers to onboard AI automation.

Looking ahead, the potential of Graiphene's approach is immense. By democratising AI access, it can level the playing field for SMEs, enabling more equitable competition with larger corporations. This democratisation signifies a shift from passive AI consumption to active application, empowering businesses to solve their problems and drive success. The journey will present challenges. The rapid pace of AI development dictates that Graiphene, like all AI products, must continuously evolve and adapt to breakthroughs. Nevertheless, historical precedent suggests that the rewards will ultimately justify the effort. Just as the internet and smartphones fundamentally transformed how we live and work, Graiphene has the potential to redefine business operations within the emerging AI age. Ultimately, AI products such as Graiphene are not merely about advanced technology; they are fundamentally about empowering people. It is about placing the transformative power of AI directly into the hands of those who stand to benefit most, thereby unlocking a future of seemingly endless possibilities.

Nevertheless, all technologies are inherently dual-natured. Their utility as invaluable tools or their peril as uncontrollable forces hinges entirely on how humans choose to deploy them. We cannot permit AI, or, critically, the humans behind its development and implementation, to operate without proper oversight and ethical considerations. Ensuring the responsible and beneficial integration of AI is paramount to harnessing its power for good while mitigating potential risks. This approach requires robust frameworks for ethical development, transparent algorithms, and mechanisms for accountability to prevent misuse and ensure that AI serves humanity's best interests. This crucial area is precisely where our attention is now focused.

NOTES

1 Bouslov, G. (2023) "From zero to GenAI chatbot hero: step-by-step guide and best practices for building advanced chatbots," https://medium.com/@gbouslov/from-zero-to-genai-chatbot-hero-29b1f45f6542. Accessed on 29 October 2024.

2 Pincents Masons (2024) "Air Canada chatbot case highlights AI liability risks," https://www.pinsentmasons.com/out-law/news/air-canada-chatbot-case-highlights-ai-liability-risks. Accessed on 29 October 2024.

3 Jyoti, R. and Schubmehl, D. (2024) "2024 Business opportunity of AI: generative AI delivering new business value and increasing ROI," https://marketingassets.microsoft.com/gdc/gdcflXNT6/original. Accessed on 16 November 2024.

4 Kopytoff, V. (2024) "This week's tech selloff shows Wall Street is getting nervous about businesses betting the bank on AI," https://fortune.com/2024/07/26/ai-spending-stocks-market-nasdaq-wall-street-alphabet-microsoft-amazon-meta/. Accessed on 15 November 2024.

5 Williams, C. (2024) "There will be no immediate productivity boost from AI," *The Economist*, 20 November, https://www.economist.com/the-world-ahead/2024/11/20/there-will-be-no-immediate-productivity-boost-from-ai. Accessed on 25 November 2024.
6 *The Economist* (2024) "Why your company is struggling to scale up generative AI," 4 November, https://www.economist.com/business/2024/11/04/why-your-company-is-struggling-to-scale-up-generative-ai. Accessed on 15 November 2024.
7 Deloitte (2024) "Now decides next: moving from potential to performance – state of generative AI in the enterprise – quarter three report," https://www2.deloitte.com/content/dam/Deloitte/us/Documents/consulting/us-state-of-gen-ai-q3.pdf. Accessed on 15 November 2024.
8 McKinsey & Company (2024) *GenAI in der fertigung angekommen – nächste welle der automatisierung mit großem potenzial* [Press release], https://www.mckinsey.de/news/presse/2024-04-22-hannover-messe-genai. Accessed on 15 November 2024.
9 El Hoyek, M., Müller, N. and Ronellenfitsch, J. (2024) "Gen AI's productivity promise: Huge potential but most have not yet reached scaled impact," https://www.mckinsey.com/capabilities/operations/our-insights/operations-blog/gen-ais-productivity-promise-huge-potential-but-most-have-not-yet-reached-scaled-impact. Accessed on 21 November 2024.
10 Deloitte (2024) "Now decides next: moving from potential to performance – state of generative AI in the enterprise - quarter three report," https://www2.deloitte.com/content/dam/Deloitte/us/Documents/consulting/us-state-of-gen-ai-q3.pdf. Accessed on 15 November 2024.
11 Daco, G. and Boussour, L. (2024) "How global business leaders can harness the power of GenAI," https://www.ey.com/en_vn/insights/ai/how-global-business-leaders-can-harness-the-power-of-gen-ai. Accessed on 21 November 2024.
12 Mischke, J., Bradley, C., Canal, M., White, O., Smit, S. and Georgieva, D. (2024) "Investing in productivity growth," https://www.mckinsey.com/mgi/our-research/investing-in-productivity-growth#/. Accessed on 15 November 2024.
13 Unfortunately, the report falls short in providing details on what constitutes "increased revenue". Deloitte (2024) "Now decides next: moving from potential to performance - state of generative AI in the enterprise - quarter three report," https://www2.deloitte.com/content/dam/Deloitte/us/Documents/consulting/us-state-of-gen-ai-q3.pdf. Accessed on 15 November 2024.
14 *The Economist* (2024) "Why your company is struggling to scale up generative AI," 4 November, https://www.economist.com/business/2024/11/04/why-your-company-is-struggling-to-scale-up-generative-ai. Accessed on 15 November 2024.
15 Deloitte (2024) "Now decides next: moving from potential to performance – state of generative AI in the enterprise – quarter three report," https://www2.deloitte.com/content/dam/Deloitte/us/Documents/consulting/us-state-of-gen-ai-q3.pdf. Accessed on 15 November 2024.

16 Deloitte (2024) "Now decides next: moving from potential to performance – state of generative AI in the enterprise – quarter three report," https://www2.deloitte.com/content/dam/Deloitte/us/Documents/consulting/us-state-of-gen-ai-q3.pdf. Accessed on 15 November 2024.
17 Jyoti, R., and Schubmehl, D. (2024) "2024 Business opportunity of AI: generative AI delivering new business value and increasing ROI," https://marketingassets.microsoft.com/gdc/gdcflXNT6/original. Accessed on 16 November 2024.
18 *The Economist* (2024) "Why your company is struggling to scale up generative AI," 4 November, https://www.economist.com/business/2024/11/04/why-your-company-is-struggling-to-scale-up-generative-ai. Accessed on 2 December 2024.
19 *The Economist* (2024) "Why your company is struggling to scale up generative AI," 4 November, https://www.economist.com/business/2024/11/04/why-your-company-is-struggling-to-scale-up-generative-ai. Accessed on 25 November 2024.
20 *The Economist* (2024) "Why your company is struggling to scale up generative AI," 4 November, https://www.economist.com/business/2024/11/04/why-your-company-is-struggling-to-scale-up-generative-ai. Accessed on 25 November 2024.
21 Jyoti, R. and Schubmehl, D. (2024) "2024 Business opportunity of AI: generative AI delivering new business value and increasing ROI," https://marketingassets.microsoft.com/gdc/gdcflXNT6/original. Accessed on 16 November 2024.
22 Deloitte (2024) "Now decides next: moving from potential to performance – state of generative AI in the enterprise – quarter three report," https://www2.deloitte.com/content/dam/Deloitte/us/Documents/consulting/us-state-of-gen-ai-q3.pdf. Accessed on 25 November 2024.
23 *The Financial Times* (2024) *AI Is Transforming the World of Work, Are We Ready for It?* [Online video], https://www.ft.com/video/fe19e874-e428-42ca-bcef-4933e59fda09. Accessed on 15 November 2024.
24 Baumeister, R. F., Bratslavsky, E., Muraven, M. and Tice, D. M. (1998) "Ego-depletion: Is the active self a limited resource?," *Journal of Personality and Social Psychology*, 18(5), pp. 130–50, https://doi.org/10.1037/0022-3514.74.5.1252. Accessed on 15 November 2024.
25 Muraven, M., Gagné, M. and Rosman, H. (2008) "Helpful Self-control: Autonomy support, vitality, and depletion," *Journal of Experimental and Social Psychology*, 44(3), pp. 573–85, https://doi.org/10.1016/j.jesp.2007.10.008. Accessed on 15 November 2024.
26 Duhigg, C. (2012) *The Power of Habit: Why We Do What We Do, and How to Change*. New York: Random House Books.
27 Bick, A., Blandin A. and Deming D. J. (2024) *The Rapid Adoption of Generative AI*. NBER Working Paper No. 32966, https://www.nber.org/system/files/working_papers/w32966/w32966.pdf. Accessed on 3 December 2024.

28 Bonney, K., Breaux, C., Buffington, C., Dinlersoz, E., Foster, L., Goldschlag, N., Haltiwanger, J., Kroff, Z. and Savage, K. (2024) *Tracking Firm Use of AI in Real Time: A Snapshot from the Business Trends and Outlook Survey*, https://www.census.gov/hfp/btos/downloads/CES-WP-24-16.pdf. Accessed on 16 August 2024.

29 Wang, G. (2019) "Humans in the loop: The design of interactive AI systems," https://hai.stanford.edu/news/humans-loop-design-interactive-ai-systems. Accessed on 9 December 2024.

30 For an in-depth treatment of the ESG problems and how AI can mitigate them, see Tse, T., Goh, D. and Esposito, M. (2020) "Using AI to achieve environmental, social and governance goals," *LSE Business Review*, 20 December, https://blogs.lse.ac.uk/businessreview/2020/12/02/using-ai-to-achieve-environmental-social-and-governance-goals/. Accessed on 26 November 2024; Tse, T., Lum, M., Goh, D. and Esposito, M. (2021) "Using AI to screen, search, and structure environmental, social, and governance data," *LSE Business Review*, 21 May, https://blogs.lse.ac.uk/businessreview/2021/05/27/using-ai-to-screen-search-and-structure-environmental-social-and-governance-data/. Accessed on 26 November 2024.

31 Credit Connect (2024) "Only one in ten SMEs regularly use AI," https://www.credit-connect.co.uk/news/only-one-in-ten-smes-regularly-use-ai/. Accessed on 28 February 2025.

CHAPTER 7

AI Native

We stand at a remarkable moment in technological history—a point where the unimaginable has become routine. Let us be honest: If we told our younger selves about the machines we now casually interact with, we would probably laugh ourselves silly. Consider the computing trajectory: At 12 years old, Danny was assembling and selling personal computers to people who were only starting to figure out their potential. Paul's excitement over Apple II's rudimentary graphics—pixels so crude they would make modern game designers weep—represented the cutting edge of digital entertainment. Terence remembers the many trips to a "station" to send telexes, mechanical contraptions that transmitted messages across continents station-to-station, a process that today would seem about as efficient as sending a message via carrier pigeon.

These are not relics of a distant past but lived experiences spanning a few decades. We have transitioned with astonishing speed from tethered, cumbersome technologies to an era of intelligent, interactive systems that would have populated the pages of science fiction just a generation ago. Midway through our professional lives, we confront a technological revolution poised to be even more transformative and disruptive than the initial digital revolution we witnessed firsthand. The second part of this book posits that we are entering the "AI-native" era—a period characterised by the fundamental restructuring of business models, the evolution of societal interactions, and the amplification of individual capabilities through deeply integrated artificial intelligence.

While precisely predicting AI's transformation is presumptuous, emerging patterns suggest accelerating, profound shifts across all sectors.

DOI: 10.1201/9781003559665-7

Reflecting on the Internet's unforeseen integral role in omnichannel strategies and mobile apps, the AI landscape will likely yield equally unimaginable innovations, dwarfing current marvels. Our aim is not prophecy but to illuminate strategic pathways by examining digital and AI advancements, offering actionable insights into this frontier. These technologies herald a profound societal and economic transformation. Fasten your seatbelts—the journey into the AI-native era promises to be intriguing and potentially game-changing.

WHAT IS AI NATIVE?

Establishing the meaning and context of a novel concept is paramount to grasping it effectively. Here, "AI native" denotes technologies, systems, or organisations fundamentally conceived, developed, and operated with artificial intelligence as their foundational core. Unlike traditional systems, where AI is often added as an additional feature or an incremental enhancement, AI-native entities are inherently driven by AI. This evolution signifies that AI is not merely an auxiliary tool but is central to its underlying architecture, core decision-making processes, and overarching functionality.

Applying the "AI-native" lens to the organisational realm describes a company or institution where AI is deeply ingrained in its core operations, permeates its cultural ethos, and informs its strategic vision from inception. These AI-native organisations leverage AI for automation and as a primary engine for driving innovation, optimising processes, enhancing human decision-making with intelligent insights, and demonstrating continuous, often real-time, adaptability to dynamic market environments. Much like the distinction between a "mobile-native" application, built specifically for mobile devices and leveraging their unique capabilities, and a "web-native" application accessed through a browser, an AI-native application will possess a fundamentally different architecture and unlock a distinct set of advantages, often characterised by intelligent automation, personalised experiences, and adaptive functionality. While some anticipate a strong synergy between AI-native applications and the decentralised infrastructure of Web 3.0, where blockchain technology supports connections, communications, and transactions, a detailed exploration of this intersection lies beyond the scope of our current discussion.

The concept of "AI native" also extends to individuals or professionals who have either grown up immersed in AI technologies or have developed a deep proficiency in their application, seamlessly integrating AI into their professional workflows and personal lives. This native fluency profoundly influences their approach to problem-solving, fosters new avenues for creativity, and significantly enhances their productivity, positioning AI as not merely a tool but an intrinsic component of their cognitive processes and operational methodologies. Ultimately, embracing an "AI-native" mindset implies a profound and inherent integration of AI into the fabric of systems, methods, or individuals, transcending its role as a simple instrument to become a fundamental and inseparable aspect of their existence and future potential.

As shown in **Figure 7.1**, each technological era has unique commercial and technological characteristics that drive societal and industrial transformation.

The Personal Computer (PC) era ushered in desktop computers and productivity software like the Microsoft Office suite into the personal workspace, catalysing a significant surge in individual productivity. This era spawned an entirely new market for hardware and subsequent portable devices and ignited the growth of a dedicated software industry, exemplified by the burgeoning PC gaming sector. Technologically, the adoption of graphical user interfaces became the standard, and the standardisation of PC hardware and operating systems enabled developers to concentrate on creating software that further enhanced user experience and personal efficiency. However, communication at this stage remained largely unidirectional: individuals interacted primarily with their local PCs.

Building upon this foundation, the Internet era profoundly reshaped the commercial landscape. The ascendance of e-commerce fundamentally

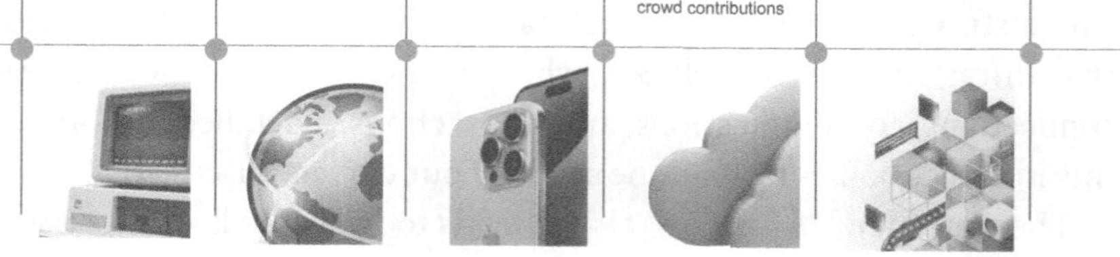

FIGURE 7.1 Technological evolution from PC to AI native.

redefined traditional retail models, creating new distribution and customer engagement avenues. Powerful search engines and comprehensive news portals revolutionised how information was accessed and disseminated globally. Technologically, websites and sophisticated web applications became ubiquitous, with HTML and web browsers emerging as essential tools. The maturation of Internet Protocol Stacks facilitated seamless global connectivity. The physical barrier between individuals and computing power diminished; with the advent of laptops, the primary separator became merely our clothing or carrying cases. Crucially, this era fostered a new dimension of human interaction, enabling widespread communication and collaboration across geographical boundaries through the Internet.

The subsequent Mobile Internet era triggered a paradigm shift with the proliferation of smartphones, igniting an explosive expansion in mobile application marketplaces. Social media platforms and mobile payment systems became mainstream, fostering an "anywhere, anytime" consumption culture and fundamentally altering consumer behaviour. Key technological advancements included the dominance of mobile operating systems like iOS and Android, characterised by intuitive touch interfaces and mobile-first design principles. The deployment of high-speed 4G networks provided the necessary mobile data infrastructure to support this shift. Notably, social media introduced the possibility of multi-way communication, enabling dynamic and interconnected interactions among users. The physical proximity to computing power became even more intimate, with handbags or pockets now representing the thin layer between individuals and their powerful mobile devices.

The cloud-native era revolutionised enterprise IT infrastructure, offering the compelling promise of reduced capital expenditure and enhanced data and information storage flexibility. The shift towards service-based models, notably Software-as-a-Service (SaaS), eliminated the necessity for massive upfront capital investments in hardware, enabling established enterprises to digitally transform and nascent start-ups to scale operations with unprecedented agility. Technologically, Infrastructure-as-a-Service (IaaS) and Platform-as-a-Service (PaaS) became foundational, with containerisation and microservices architectures emerging as the new standard, delivering seamless scalability and operational flexibility within cloud environments. However, this paradigm shift introduced a new layer of dependency, with companies and individuals now relying not only on traditional software and hardware providers but also on the robustness and security of the underlying cloud infrastructure. This era also ushered in the potential for one-to-many communication through platform communities, leveraging the crowd's collective intelligence and contributions.

We now stand on the cusp of the AI-native era, where data transcends its traditional role to become a core, strategic business asset. The confluence of exponentially increasing data generation and sophisticated algorithms that transform unstructured data into actionable insights is driving a new wave of personalised services and predictive analytics, fundamentally reshaping business decision-making processes and customer experiences. AI is beginning to dismantle traditional labour structures, streamlining workflows and compressing the timelines associated with established methods. The defining technological characteristic of this era is the deep integration of large language models (LLMs) directly into products and services, synergistically combining AI and big data technologies to unlock the potential of processing vast, complex datasets. Automation and embedded intelligence are rapidly becoming the new benchmarks in software development and business operations.

Viewed in historical context, each technological revolution—from the advent of personal computers and the rise of the Internet to the mobile Internet and cloud computing—represents a significant technological advancement and a fundamental transformation of business models, social interactions, and work methodologies. However, the AI-native era signifies a shift of a different magnitude. The emergent technologies are not merely reshaping our world once again; they are altering how we have operated and lived for the past several decades, challenging long-held assumptions and demanding a fundamental rethinking of strategy, talent, and competition.

THE UNCHANGING NATURE OF DECISION-MAKING

The act of human decision-making is a fundamental thread woven throughout our existence, shaping our personal lives and professional endeavours as a continuous stream of choices, each informed by those that preceded it. While seemingly intuitive, the concept of decision-making transcends a simple definition, yet at its core, it represents the critical process of selecting a course of action from multiple possibilities. These choices arise from a complex interplay of both rational analysis and often subconscious, even irrational, influences, profoundly shaped by our values, ingrained preferences, and firmly held beliefs, drawing upon both explicit knowledge we can readily articulate and a tacit understanding that operates beneath the surface of our conscious awareness.

Throughout history, our relationship with data has served as an indispensable foundation for this decision-making process. From the earliest inscriptions on papyrus, humanity has diligently recorded information, constructing an ever-expanding knowledge repository. As our capacity for data accumulation surged, so too did the physical manifestation of this information, evolving into towering stacks of paper that became potent symbols of both the intellectual capital they contained and the cognitive burden they represented. This historical context underscores the enduring human quest to leverage information in navigating complexity and making informed choices. This quest continues to evolve dramatically in the face of the modern data deluge.

The PC era heralded a monumental shift in our relationship with data, igniting the great digitalisation of information. The transition from cumbersome paper records to the fluid realm of digital storage represents a remarkable acceleration of technological evolution: from the early days of clunky metal boxes housing fragile floppy disk drives to increasingly robust and capacious storage solutions. This progression reached a symbolic zenith with the iconic 1994 photograph of Bill Gates towering over two immense columns of paper, visually demonstrating the staggering data density achievable by a single CD-ROM. Parallel to this exponential growth in storage capacity, the physical embodiment of computing power underwent a radical metamorphosis—from bulky desktop PCs tethered to a single location to streamlined laptops offering portability and ultimately culminating in the ubiquitous smartphones that now reside in the palms of our hands, each containing more information than the legendary ancient Library of Alexandria.[1]

Nevertheless, despite this revolutionary transformation in storing and accessing information, the fundamental cognitive pathway of human decision-making has remained remarkably static. We largely adhere to the same time-intensive process of reading, absorbing, comprehending, and analysing information, often repetitively, to arrive at a choice. This enduring reliance on traditional decision-making patterns is starkly illustrated by the commonplace dilemma of selecting a ride-sharing service. Consider the scenario of a busy professional rushing between meetings, acutely aware of time constraints and budget considerations. The typical response involves opening multiple apps offering essentially the same service, laboriously comparing estimated arrival times ***and*** pricing—the internal debate often boiling down to a granular trade-off: "Is a marginal one-minute difference in arrival worth a premium fare?" This same iterative evaluation will likely be repeated for every subsequent meeting and engagement.

While we have successfully miniaturised our data storage capabilities and engineered digital alternatives to traditional services—replacing the unpredictability of hailing a street taxi with the comparative certainty of ride-sharing apps—the underlying mechanism of our decision-making process remains largely unaltered. Despite the impressive computational power surrounding us, our digital tools remain largely passive participants in this crucial process. They await our explicit instructions rather than proactively transforming how we arrive at decisions. It is possible to visualise our decision-making process as the cone shown in the upper part of **Figure 7.2**, having to boil down a great deal of data to decide to instruct machines to carry out our wishes.

This persistence of traditional decision-making patterns in an age of unprecedented technological capability raises essential questions about the future of human-machine interaction and decision support. While we have made remarkable progress in data storage and access, the cognitive burden of decision-making rests squarely on human shoulders. We believe the AI-native era is finally changing the latter.

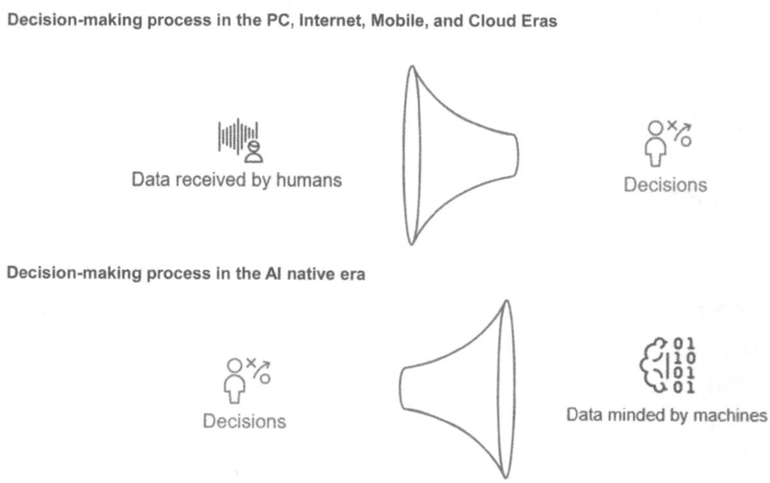

FIGURE 7.2 Decision-making process in the AI-native era.

AI NATIVE DECISION-MAKING

The decision-making landscape faces a profound, irreversible shift driven by the convergence of predictive analytics, NLP, and generative AI. These technologies fundamentally reshape data interaction and decision architecture, transcending traditional methods. Intelligent algorithms now autonomously gather, parse, and process vast data to generate optimal choices, often anticipating needs proactively. This ability promises unprecedented efficiency and accelerated strategic agility and empowers organisations to make more informed, timely decisions in an increasingly complex, data-rich world. This phenomenon represents a dramatic shift in the decision-making process, effectively inverting the traditional cone-shaped model and significantly compressing the time required to reach decisions, similar to the lower part of **Figure 7.2**.

The profound implications of this shift become strikingly clear when we reimagine familiar scenarios through the lens of proactive intelligence. Consider the everyday friction of hailing a ride: intelligent algorithms could seamlessly synthesise data from your email and calendar to anticipate crucial client meetings, analyse your real-time location and destination requirements, dynamically compare arrival times and pricing across all available ride-sharing platforms, and even factor in your historical spending patterns gleaned from banking data. The system could then autonomously execute a booking that precisely aligns with your preferences and priorities, ensuring a timely arrival at your next client meeting without manual comparison or decision fatigue.

This predictive paradigm extends beyond simple transportation logistics to address more intricate scenarios. Envision the optimisation of airport travel planning: advanced algorithms could synthesise real-time traffic conditions, compare pricing across a range of transportation options (from ride-sharing to airport express trains), and intelligently incorporate your typical airport behaviour—whether you prioritise business lounge access or prefer to proceed directly to the departure gate—to calculate the optimal departure time from your location. The outcome is a perfectly orchestrated journey that alleviates the stress of potential delays and the unproductive downtime of excessive early arrival while adhering to your preferred budget parameters. In this evolved paradigm, the role of human decision-making transitions from active, often tedious, selection to a more strategic evaluation and validation of machine-generated recommendations, freeing up valuable cognitive resources for higher-level tasks. The traditionally elongated and cumbersome decision-making process has been inverted and significantly compressed, representing a dramatically accelerated path from raw data to informed action.

This proactive intelligence fundamentally reshapes business-customer tech interaction and critical decisions. For businesses, AI evolves into a proactive decision-making partner. Instead of just presenting data, sophisticated AI analyses user behaviour to offer personalised recommendations and pre-emptive solutions, becoming an active part of core operations. Just as databases are now foundational, sophisticated machine learning will be seamlessly integrated into all future business software, making intelligent automation and predictive insights inherent features driving organisational efficiency and strategic advantage.

A key breakthrough lies in AI's real-time processing of unstructured data—emails, documents, conversations—enabling unprecedented speed in anticipating customer needs and market shifts. This capability fuels a fundamental change in customer engagement: moving beyond mass interactions on platforms (like social media) towards truly personalised one-to-one relationships at scale, where each customer experiences a uniquely tailored interaction.

This personalisation engine creates novel business opportunities, akin to how cloud computing catalysed the SaaS revolution. The crucial distinction is that instead of users adapting to a product's interface, AI-powered offerings will dynamically adjust to individual user workflows and behaviours, drastically reducing friction and accelerating adoption. This capability necessitates a paradigm shift in how business leaders conceive and deliver products and services. The future belongs to those who strategically leverage AI to craft adaptive, deeply personalised experiences, moving decisively away from outdated one-size-fits-all models.

BUSINESS IN THE AI-NATIVE ERA

We are not fully there yet, but the trajectory is clear. Whether standalone or integrated, today's GenAI is evolving into a sophisticated task automation engine, increasingly capable of informing decision-making. Consider its application in the complex realm of ESG investing. The core challenge of ESG lies in its inherent ambiguity—a universally accepted definition remains elusive. Nevertheless, financial services (and other sectors like retail and academia) are urgently pursuing ESG initiatives, necessitating each financial services company to develop its proprietary methodology for assessing ESG compliance. It typically requires answers to anywhere from 40 to 200 qualifying questions, with a standard 60-question assessment demanding an extraordinary 5–6 months of manual compilation.

The enduring reliance on traditional methods, notably Excel spreadsheets, highlights a deeper challenge in tech adoption. Past efforts to modernise these processes with centralised systems and standardised interfaces have met significant resistance. Despite potential gains, users consistently favour Excel's familiar flexibility—easy row/column manipulation and data reorganisation—over learning new platforms. This inertia maintains the status quo, with teams worldwide clinging to spreadsheets despite their inherent limitations. This challenge intensifies in global operations. Regional teams—EMEA, Asia, and the Americas—maintain disparate ESG criteria and inquiries, reflecting unique market conditions and regulations. This fragmentation hinders standardisation, escalates complexity, and increases the sheer volume of questions as each region retains its distinct definitions and concerns.

However, a revolutionary approach is emerging: leveraging LLMs to create prompts that elicit and process data, automatically generating responses to extensive question lists and populating familiar Excel spreadsheets. This approach preserves user comfort with their spreadsheet environment while fundamentally transforming underlying data gathering and processing. This transformation necessitates robust data traceability, with AI systems meticulously recording information sources for all ESG answers.

This innovative approach fundamentally reshapes ESG professionals' workflows. Instead of doing manual research and answering individual questions, staff can concentrate on refining the quality and accuracy of AI-generated responses within their familiar tools. This human-in-the-loop model ensures continuous algorithmic improvement while upholding the reliability of ESG assessments. By embracing this shift, organisations can significantly scale their ESG analysis capabilities without disrupting established team workflows.

AGENTIC AI

GenAI has reached a critical juncture. Despite recent explosive demand, its standalone application may be plateauing in terms of actionable business value. While LLMs excel at content generation, their capacity to deliver direct, integrated intelligence within existing business workflows remains limited.[2] Nevertheless, businesses and technology providers do not stand still just because a technology has reached its limit. Inevitably, the next step is combining different technologies to open up new opportunities.[3]

Enter agentic AI.

We are transitioning from passive AI tools towards combining AI, automation, diverse software, and human expertise to execute complex autonomous workflows. Unlike traditional AI, which is bound by fixed rules and requires explicit instruction for each step, and GenAI, adept at content creation based on prompts, agentic AI marks a significant advancement. It can independently execute tasks and make decisions to achieve defined objectives.

Consider the following cooking analogy. Traditional AI is like a cookbook. It provides recipes and instructions, but you need to follow them step-by-step. GenAI, on the other hand, works like a recipe generator. You can input your preferences, and it will generate a new recipe tailored to your tastes. In contrast, agentic AI is akin to a personal chef. You state what you want, and the chef takes care of everything, from planning the menu to cooking and serving it.

Three fundamental attributes characterise AI agents:

- Autonomy: Agentic AI systems autonomously execute complex tasks towards high-level objectives like supply chain optimisation or customer relationship management, independently determining and implementing necessary steps. While operating with significant autonomy, they are designed to defer to human oversight for critical decisions, ensuring appropriate control over sensitive operations.
- Adaptability: A defining characteristic of agentic AI is its inherent capacity for systematic learning and adaptation. These systems continuously refine their performance by analysing the outcomes of their actions and integrating new data streams. For example, in customer service, an agentic AI progressively enhances its response patterns based on the history of interactions and the measured success of those engagements. This iterative learning loop enables increasingly sophisticated and effective operations, leading to more nuanced and context-aware interactions.
- Goal orientation: Unlike reactive or purely generative systems, agentic AI operates with purposeful direction towards specific objectives. Given a business goal like improving operational efficiency, these systems analyse conditions, identify opportunities, develop strategies, and implement solutions, ensuring all actions align with intended outcomes.

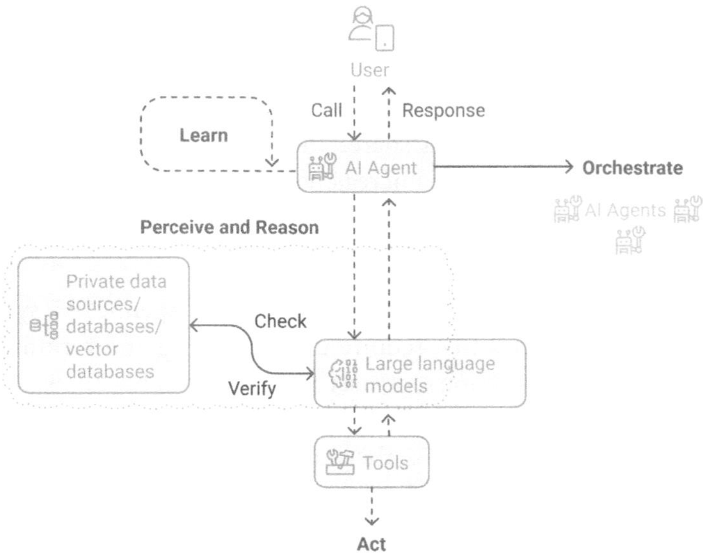

FIGURE 7.3 An overview of how agentic AI works.

These attributes position agentic AI as a powerful "do-it-yourself" catalyst, propelling us into the next generation of the "do-it-for-me" economy. This transition has the potential to fundamentally reshape user access to services and the overall market structure. Just as the Internet era revolutionised the economy and society, AI is poised to drive even more profound transformations, particularly agentic AI.[4] Let us break down an AI agent's steps, as shown in **Figure 7.3**.

1. Perceiving: An agent gathers and processes data from various information sources.
2. Reasoning: It uses GenAI to understand tasks, generate solutions, and coordinate specialised AI models for specific functions such as content creation and recommendation systems.
3. Acting: The agent executes tasks using various tools, such as spreadsheets or customised user interfaces, based on the goal to be reached. What makes agentic AI very powerful is, therefore, these two steps that enable an agent to "ReAct"—**re**asoning and **act**ing.
4. Learning: The agent improves its performance through feedback and experience, becoming more effective and efficient in making

decisions over time. This is made possible by memory, remembering past questions, user intent and even subtle contextual clues to provide relevant or repetitive responses.

5. Orchestrating: An agent shares information and collaborates with other AI agents to solve increasingly complex problems, delivering better user performance.

It is important to note that memory enables agentic AI systems to engage in complex tasks that require understanding and recalling previous interactions, instructions, or user preferences. This allows the agent to go beyond simple, pre-programmed responses and act autonomously in changing environments. Furthermore, memory allows AI agents to remember user preferences, behaviours, and goals, enabling tailored and human-like interactions. Lastly, agentic AI can better recognise anomalies, anticipate future events, and perform multi-step reasoning by recalling historical data and patterns with memory.

Overall, an AI agent functions like a highly skilled personal assistant who understands objectives and proactively works towards achieving them without constant direction. Implementing agentic AI is a strategic leap, offering sophisticated automation with vital human oversight, boosting efficiency, and preserving judgement in key decisions. This balanced approach aligns advanced AI with strategic goals and governance, synergising technology and human control for optimal performance.

This novel AI technology diverges from GenAI in crucial aspects. While GenAI excels in content creation, agentic AI prioritises autonomous decision-making and goal attainment. GenAI typically relies on human prompts for output. In contrast, agentic AI operates with greater independence, charting its course to achieve objectives by executing complex action sequences, independently sourcing data, and triggering workflows—capabilities beyond mere content generation.[5] Put differently, the key features of this latest form of AI are autonomy (as it can operate without continuous human guidance, performing tasks on its own), adaptability (because these systems will learn from interactions, receive feedback, and adjust their decisions based on what they have learned), and goal orientation (as the algorithm is programmed with clear objectives and can reason about how to achieve specific tasks).[6]

Agentic AI is a significant jump forward in AI capabilities. While traditional AI and GenAI are valuable tools, agentic AI takes algorithms to the next level by empowering them to act independently and achieve specific goals. To illustrate this progression, from this vantage point, agentic AI is poised to revolutionise business operations across industries from several perspectives, including:

Boosting efficiency: Imagine AI agents streamlining finance, healthcare, and logistics tasks, reducing costs and freeing employees for strategic work. Agentic AI can automate complex processes, manage inventory, and handle administrative burdens like patient data management.

Making smarter decisions: AI agents can analyse vast datasets, providing valuable insights for faster and more accurate decision-making. From market trend monitoring to dynamic strategy adjustments, agentic AI can empower businesses to stay ahead of the curve.

Personalising customer experiences: This can take the form of 24/7 AI-powered chatbots, customised services, and even the potential for AI agents to handle a significant portion of digital storefront interactions.

Developing innovation and new products: Agentic AI can make highly personalised robo-advisors, adaptive asset management systems, or even AI-powered micro-insurance products possible. Additionally, AI agent integration into enterprise software applications is expected to rise significantly.

Enhancing risk management: Agentic AI performs risk assessments in real-time, allowing for proactive responses to emerging threats. This capability can potentially translate to improved fraud detection, autonomous trading in finance, and enhanced cybersecurity through continuous monitoring.

RESHAPING LIVES

The accessibility of AI agents is rapidly increasing and is driven by continuously improving development tools. AI agents are no longer solely for corporations; individuals can now create basic agents with minimal coding expertise. Furthermore, the cost of building these agents is set to decrease. The emergence of open-source LLMs like DeepSeek offers a more affordable alternative to the expensive, closed models developed by US tech giants. Additionally, like those technological advancements in the

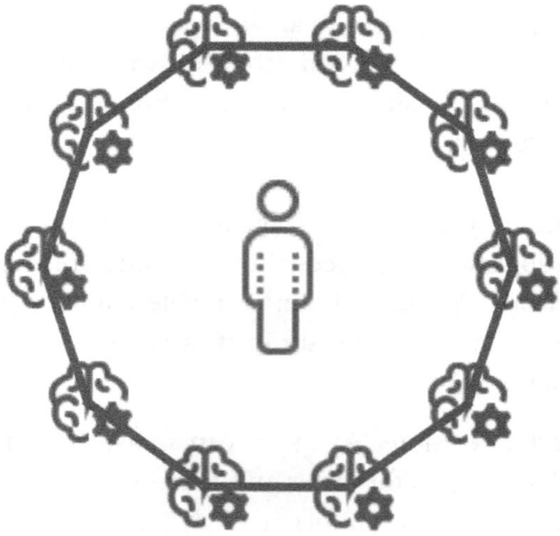

FIGURE 7.4 Individuals will be able to deploy multiple AI agents.

past, there will be more and more tools at the application level to quickly build and put such agents into use. The result: we will be building many AI agents around us that can take on different tasks and work with each other, a depiction of which is in **Figure 7.4**.

The ease, speed, and affordability of creating AI agents will impact our daily lives. Consider the following example: instead of us manually checking the different apps, including maps, ride-hailing apps, and train schedules in a coordinated fashion, AI agents can orchestrate the entire process on our behalf. A practical scenario would involve an AI agent determining the fastest route home. AI can work out the best commuter train for a user to take when leaving her workplace, arrange for a taxi to be waiting upon arrival at the station closest to her home, and continuously update the plan to accommodate any delays. This situation is not hypothetical; in Shanghai, Baidu already offers a glimpse of a real-time service that manages such logistics.

Furthermore, it does not have to stop here: AI agents could ensure dinner is delivered to the doorstep just as she arrives home. Essentially, this is "applifying" separate tasks at the individual level, with multiple AI-powered applications working together seamlessly towards achieving a given goal: making it easy for her to get home and providing a smooth transition to her evening. Over time, it will not be extended to think that AI agents are taking over more of the routine and tedious tasks humans must currently handle. People will be surrounded by a growing network of AI tools that manage their daily routine, undertakings, and chores.

The implications of this transformation are substantial. One key aspect of agentic AI is that the agents can communicate and collaborate, thereby eliminating the necessity for individuals to engage with companies directly. Rather than us interacting with machines, the paradigm is shifting towards machines communicating with other machines on our behalf. In the ride-sharing scenario, a person no longer needs to check a mapping app for train arrival times and then switch to a ride-hailing app to book a car. Machine-to-machine communications will effectively render traditional user interfaces obsolete. This phenomenon is not new: we have evolved from handwriting to typewriting, from keyboards to voice commands. The medium of input has transformed over time. The next stage may see interfaces vanish entirely. Companies that depend on sleek user interfaces will no longer be able to leverage them as a key differentiator. As a result, platform businesses—companies that mediate exchanges between customers and providers—face the risk of diminishing relevance or becoming obsolete. Rather than depending on a platform to locate a counterparty, AI agents can proactively identify and directly engage with appropriate counterparts.

AI agents will optimise the use of personal data in ways that go far beyond current personalisation efforts. At present, individuals must explicitly declare their preferences before receiving recommendations. Customers are often asked for their cuisine preference when ordering food on an app. On some airlines, passengers can specify their choice of an aisle seat. With AI agents capable of integrating and analysing all available data, this manual input becomes unnecessary. For instance, an AI agent would not only ensure that dinner is delivered to you as you step out of the taxi, but it would also predict the most appealing meal choice based on previous meals, thus removing the need to decide among Indian, Chinese, or Italian cuisine. Your selection of aisle seats on the past ten flights provides sufficient grounds for the AI agent to know that you prefer such a seat when travelling. AI agents are evolving to anticipate personal needs, both expressed and unspoken.

FROM ATTENTION TO INTENTION TO INTIMACY

Our friend John Beck (together with Thomas Davenport) was among the first to describe the online world as the "attention economy."[7] They argued that capturing and holding consumer attention was crucial for online business success. With AI's increasing ability to predict and, more importantly, direct our needs, businesses must operate in the "intention economy," where motivations become currency. Companies can monetise "intention" by finding subtle ways to manipulate and influence motivations; these approaches include mirroring users' linguistic style to foster a sense of familiarity or predicting their likely statements based on the patterns observed in similar user groups.[8]

In the AI-native era, intimacy is another currency emerging alongside intention. As historian Yuval Harari notes, the AI revolution shifts competition from capturing attention to deeply understanding and responding to individuals.[9] Intimacy goes deeper than attention; it can change our views, shape our minds, and influence our decisions and behaviour.

This shift is already taking place in two ways. As mentioned above, over the past six decades, computing power has become an inseparable part of our lives, from laptops to mobile phones to brain-computer interfaces. We suspect that traditional input methods such as buttons and keypads will become obsolete sooner or later in an era characterised by heavy use of AI agents. As AI manages our daily tasks, it becomes increasingly intimate by learning our preferences, exerting a far more potent influence than mere attention. While deep relationships were once exclusive to humans and animals, individuals are now forming long-term romantic connections with machines.[10] In June 2022, Blake Lemoine, a Google engineer working on the AI chatbot LaMDA, made headlines by publicly declaring that the system had achieved sentience. This controversial assertion ultimately led to his dismissal from the company. What stands out most about this incident is not Lemoine's likely unfounded claim of AI consciousness. Instead, it is his willingness to sacrifice his well-paying job at Google to advocate for what he believed was a sentient AI entity.[11] If AI can convince someone to quit their job, what else can it do to influence us?

Algorithmic intimacy raises significant ethical concerns related to privacy, manipulation, and the potential for businesses to exploit human vulnerabilities for profit through mass-manufactured connections. However, the advent of AI agents, serving as personal advocates, may provide a powerful countermeasure. By coordinating and synchronising vast amounts of user data to achieve optimal individual outcomes, these agents can function as effective gatekeepers, releasing only the minimum necessary data to businesses in exchange for services.[12]

Consider this issue: whenever you use single sign-on, you allow your data to be shared with the website, often more than you might realise. Since setting this up is so effortless, you could unknowingly grant broader access than intended. While platforms are willing to let you review and remove third-party connections, revoking access does not necessarily mean the website stops using your data—the website retains your information. If you return to the same site and log in with your social account again, it is as if you never revoked access in the first place.[13] Using the default browser setting, users allegedly give a lot of personal data away.[14] With our data synchronised and in firm control by the user (by the AI agents, to be more precise), we may find ourselves not to be quickly taken advantage of by companies' data mining initiatives. Indeed, driven by profit, tech companies will undoubtedly find ways to circumvent this. Nevertheless, at least we can protect our data, and the resistance is no longer a lopsided affair favouring these businesses.

THE DEPARTMENT OF ONE

The impact of AI agents extends beyond individual users to businesses. One observable development direction is at Nexus FrontierTech, where marketing once required an entire team of employees. With AI-driven tools, similar results can now be achieved by just two people, representing only a fraction of the cost. At Google, more than 25% of newly generated code is already written by AI. It is natural to assume that AI-native companies will require fewer employees to achieve the same outputs, if not more significant ones, as these tools become more advanced. With the increase in the use of AI agents, we are likely moving towards a "department of one"—where tasks that previously needed an entire team can now be completed by a single person leveraging AI. This situation echoes the view of Nvidia's Jensen Huang when he recently commented that "we are all going to be CEOs of AI agents."[15] AI agents are a boon for start-ups constantly fighting drawn-out battles with costs. Cloud computing increases operational leverage by converting capital expenditures into operating expenditures. Agentic AI could hyperscale operating expenditures, potentially powering a golden age for these companies.[16] Arguably, we might one day see a "unicorn of one."

What about the workers themselves? An initial concern is job displacement due to AI agents. However, we anticipate a significant near-term impact: the reversal of offshoring trends. Labour costs have historically driven corporations to outsource to lower-wage countries. Nevertheless,

AI agents, capable of performing labour-intensive tasks more efficiently and cost-effectively than offshore human workers, will likely incentivise companies to bring back previously outsourced activities. While low-labour-cost economies may experience economic repercussions, high-cost economies stand to benefit from domestic job creation. Although this transformation may unfold over the next decade, a radical reshaping of the workplace is inevitable, demanding a proactive rethinking of workforce training and skill development strategies.

BLOCKBUSTER 2: NETFLIX 1

Let us debunk a popular misconception. Since Joseph Schumpeter introduced the idea of "creative disruption," we have been conditioned to believe that new technologies inevitably overthrow established players, paving the way for a new generation of market leaders. It is often too easy to assume that the current AI revolution will follow the same trajectory as the software/IT revolution. Values have historically flowed from lower-tech businesses to higher-tech new entrants in previous industrial revolutions. Handmade workshops gave way to machine-filled factories. Car makers and garages displaced horse breeders, stable hands, and farriers. The headline transformation of the software/IT revolution was undoubtedly the value transfer from analogue to digital businesses. The e-commerce era also saw new players dismantling many market incumbents. At the rate AI technologies are evolving, we may be looking at a market turned upside down in the future—incumbents will reign. Unlike the previous waves of disruption, Blockbuster could surpass Netflix, taxi medallions could outsmart Uber, and Accenture or McKinsey could prove more resilient than Palantir. To be clear, AI is not rewriting history—it will not bring back Blockbuster or restore the dominance of taxi medallions. The point is that those who rely on outdated heuristics suggesting that disruptors will always replace their traditional counterparts may want to consider supporting the incumbents instead.

The inherent strengths of established companies should not be underestimated. Incumbents possess key assets that offer a significant advantage in the AI era. Firstly, they often have extensive datasets. As discussed previously, well-managed data is a critical fuel for AI adoption. Secondly, established players can leverage their profound domain expertise to fundamentally rethink and reinvent their existing processes and workforce structures. While start-ups may boast technological prowess, they often lack the nuanced domain knowledge necessary for developing impactful products. Thirdly, incumbents typically wield greater financial power, providing the capital required for substantial AI-driven transformations.

The fintech industry offers a compelling illustration. Initially, many fintech start-ups garnered praise for their ability to capture market share from traditional banks with sleek interfaces and highly automated processes. However, in recent years, legacy banks have demonstrated a notable resurgence. Higher interest rates have bolstered their capital reserves, providing the necessary funds for strategic technology investments, particularly in AI. Furthermore, traditional banks benefit from extensive existing customer bases, making cross-selling and migrating to digital platforms more cost-effective.[17] The initial advantage of fintechs, often specialising in narrow product ranges, has also proven challenging for sustained profitability, compelling many to broaden their offerings, thus diminishing their differentiation from established competitors.

With the rise of agentic AI, incumbents can reclaim their leadership positions, avoiding the fates of Kodak, Blockbuster, and even Intel. AI enables these established businesses to operate with the same speed, efficiency, and cost-effectiveness as their newer rivals, allowing them to set market trends rather than react to them.

One business model that has seen remarkable growth is the platform business, and legacy companies have been recommended to adopt it for better competition.[18] However, its dominance in the AI-native era is questionable. As AI agents gain the ability to interact with service providers directly, the need for intermediaries connecting supply and demand diminishes. An AI agent can determine what you want for dinner and order food directly from a restaurant. In that situation, there is little reason to rely on food delivery platforms that centralise different restaurant options under a single URL. Similarly, ride-sharing businesses may become obsolete when AI agents can directly negotiate with the most cost-effective driver, bypassing the need for a platform.

While the demand side faces potential fragmentation, the supply side of these platforms is also less stable than it appears. Many drivers operate across multiple ride-hailing apps simultaneously to maximise earnings, weakening the control of any single platform. If AI agents further automate this multi-platform engagement for drivers, the foundational strength of platform-based businesses will erode even faster. The collapse of these platforms could be swift. While their success is often attributed to network effects, innovation, and user experience,[19] much of their *financial* success stems from keeping labour costs very low, so low that repeated reports have revealed the deplorable conditions gig workers often face.[20] As platform revenues potentially shrink in the AI-native era, the pressure to further reduce costs will likely intensify, making these platforms less attractive to workers. AI may well accelerate the decline of the platform business model as we currently know it.

HUMAN CONTEXT WINDOWS

With the future business and social landscapes potentially changing significantly, the skills required to thrive in the new setting could differ considerably from those needed today. Looking at the skills employers believe to be important in the coming few years could hint at the most critical skills (see sidebar).[21] A recent survey ranked technology skills as a top priority. This finding is unsurprising given the stellar rise of AI technologies.

The nature of "technology skills" will fundamentally evolve in the AI-native era. The barriers to building AI applications are rapidly dissolving. Developers are increasingly freed from intricate coding, as many platforms offer intuitive, drag-and-drop interfaces, empowering even non-programmers to create AI-powered systems. Tools like Graiphene enable SMEs to integrate AI into their workflows without writing code. Technical AI development prowess is no longer scarce but an increasingly democratised asset.

The rise of AI agents will necessitate a shift in required technology skills, potentially replacing the emphasis on "AI and big data" with expertise in "overseeing and enhancing AI agents." Concurrently, cognitive skills and self-efficacy will likely become more critical. AI agents are extensions of their human controllers; their output quality is ultimately determined not by the software itself but by the intellectual depth, curiosity, values, and ethical framework of the individual at the centre. These agents are not autonomous entities but rather reflections of their creators. As the saying goes, "a chain is only as strong as its weakest link," underscoring the importance of continuous self-improvement for effective AI agent utilisation.

SKILLS ON THE RISE (2025–2030)

The below table shows the skills that employers consider important in the near future. Skills are ranked based on net increase, which is the difference between the share of surveyed employers that consider a skill category to be increasing in use and those that believe it to be decreasing in use.

Skills	Net increase	Skill clusters
1. AI and big data	87	Technology skills
2. Networks and cybersecurity	70	Technology skills
3. Technological literacy	68	Technology skills
4. Creative thinking	66	Cognitive skills
5. Resilience, flexibility and agility	66	Self-efficacy
6. Curiosity and lifelong learning	61	Self-efficacy
7. Leadership and social influence	58	Working with others
8. Talent management	58	Management skills
9. Analytical thinking	55	Cognitive skills
10. Environmental stewardship	53	Ethics

Source: World Economic Forum (2025) Future of Jobs Report 2025, January.

Let us introduce a new idea: the "human context windows." In AI, the "context window" defines the amount of information a model can process simultaneously. Gemini 1.5, for instance, could process one million tokens, whereas Gemini 1.5 Pro could handle two million tokens.[22] A wider context window allows AI models to synthesise more information, analyse larger datasets, and generate more nuanced insights.

Similarly, humans possess their context windows—our capacity to absorb, reflect upon, and synthesise information affects the depth and breadth of our intellectual engagement. Expanding our personal context window enhances our ability to navigate complexity, identify interdisciplinary connections, and anticipate long-term and systemic consequences.

A recent conversation illustrated this vividly. Speaking with a UK-based R&D funding consultant, Danny was repeatedly asked whether Nexus FrontierTech was building an LLM. Despite numerous explanations that constructing an LLM today requires billions of dollars, far beyond their means, the consultant remained fixated on the idea. His rigid mental framework led him to believe that AI innovation was synonymous with LLM development, closing his eyes to the broader landscape of AI applications and developments. Paradoxically, at the very moment when we need to expand our intellectual horizons, the forces of modern technology—particularly social media—are conspiring to shrink them.

Increasingly, we observe students whose engagement in the classroom struggles to extend beyond the immediate gratification of social media, showing reluctance for deep thinking and presence. While conclusive empirical evidence on social media's direct impact on intelligence remains debated, its detrimental effects on cognitive depth are increasingly apparent. Excessive use has been correlated with heightened loneliness, diminished self-esteem, reduced life satisfaction, and increased anxiety.[23] Alarmingly, it can also foster impulsivity, erode empathy, fragment self-identity, and disrupt crucial sleep patterns.[24] The impact on younger generations is particularly concerning. It is perhaps no accident that "Wireless Mobile Devices" share the same initials as "Weapons of Mass Destruction."

We would be far better served by engaging with the sustained focus required by reading than by the fragmented attention fostered by mindless social media scrolling. Conscious and continuous effort must be directed towards expanding our intellectual context window. Indeed, as agentic AI shifts the economic drivers of business from employee payroll to software subscriptions, the humans at the centre of these AI agent networks must cultivate and expand their cognitive capacities.

As AI reshapes the economy, the defining competitive advantage will not reside in the technical skill of manipulating code but rather in the breadth of one's context window, encompassing diverse perspectives, nuanced insights, and the disciplined capacity to grapple with complexity. Those who neglect the cultivation of these human attributes risk being outpaced, not by the machines themselves, but by those individuals who have mastered the art of wielding them with profound understanding and strategic foresight.

"SPECIALIST" LANGUAGE MODELS

As previously discussed, GenAI's value as a standalone technology may be reaching a plateau, likely leading to its evolution from a direct application to a foundational infrastructure layer within the broader AI landscape. Concurrently, AI agents are anticipated to develop towards increasing specialisation, each meticulously engineered for peak performance in a single, clearly defined task. This trend will likely drive demand for scaled-down, leaner, and more efficient GenAI models—the so-called small language models (SLMs).

SLMs offer distinct advantages over their larger counterparts. Their compact size allows for precise fine-tuning for specific tasks or industry domains, rendering them exceptionally adept at handling narrow applications with superior accuracy. Unlike LLMs, which often function as generalists with broad capabilities but potentially less focused expertise, these optimised models deliver enhanced precision and efficiency within their designated areas of operation. Therefore, SLMs are not merely miniaturised LLMs; they are purpose-built engines optimised for excellence in specific domains. Their reduced computational footprint also translates to significantly faster response times, a critical advantage for real-time applications where even fractions of a second can be decisive.

The dominance of costly, proprietary LLMs—often monopolised by Silicon Valley's tech titans—is already facing formidable challengers. DeepSeek has demonstrated that high-performing language models can be built affordably without excessive computational overhead. By reducing the precision of numerical processing from 32 decimal places to just eight (known as "quantisation"), DeepSeek slashes memory requirements by a staggering 75%. (This is not very different from using 3.14 as π instead of 3.1415926535 to calculate the circumference of a circle—you get an excellent estimate, but much faster). Meanwhile, its innovative approach of reading entire phrases rather than processing words sequentially has doubled efficiency while maintaining 90% of the original model's accuracy. It also uses "distillation," a technique that trains smaller, more efficient models by learning from larger, more complex ones. Instead of making a new AI learn from scratch, a powerful "teacher" model produces answers and insights, which a smaller "student" model will then study and mimic. This process drastically reduces computing costs while maintaining strong performance, allowing AI to run faster and more affordably. All these enabled DeepSeek to train a model that can compete with the latest version of ChatGPT for $6 million.

The notion that building high-calibre AI demands astronomical budgets is further unravelling. In January 2025, researchers at UC Berkeley built a reasoning model that can rival an older version of ChatGPT for just $450.[25] The following month, another research team in the United States—including Li Fei-Fei, the so-called "Godmother of AI"—trained a high-performing language model for as little as $50. The model, trained for a mere 26 minutes on 16 Nvidia H100 GPUs (rented for as little as $2 per hour), outperformed a recent OpenAI system on targeted tasks by fine-tuning Qwen.[26] Granted, these cheaper models cannot be compared like-for-like with the LLMs. Nevertheless, these milestones signal a paradigm shift: while all-purpose, robust, cutting-edge AI remains the exclusive domain of trillion-dollar enterprises, independent researchers and start-ups are increasingly able to develop smaller, more efficient models without the massive outlay and computing costs.

Beyond speed and cost, SLMs offer crucial autonomy and function offline, unlike cloud-dependent LLMs; this ability will make SLMs vital in areas with poor connectivity, continuing AI's role in alleviating the inequalities between developed and developing nations.[27] Imagine instant, private on-device intelligence. SLMs also mitigate LLM issues like hallucinations by training on focused, high-quality data, yielding more accurate results. While LLMs remain a broad AI infrastructure, SLMs will proliferate with agentic AI. Developers will leverage larger models to create lightweight, fast, specialised SLMs for specific agent needs, like a fraud detection agent needing no customer interaction. The next AI frontier is sharper, leaner, purpose-driven intelligence, making the AI-native era both vast and precise.

We are entering the AI-native era, enabled by agentic AI, promising significant benefits for companies, societies, and individuals. However, the path to this prosperity will be challenging, with substantial problems to overcome. The next chapter will focus on the critical risks and challenges we must address to ensure responsible AI development and deployment.

NOTES

1 It has been estimated that the Library of Alexandria contained about 12.5 gigabytes of information. Robertson, D. S. (1990) "The information revolution," *Communication Research*, 17(2), pp. 235–54, https://doi.org/10.1177/009365090017002005. An entry-level mobile phone often starts with 16 gigabytes.

2 Davenport, T. H. and Barkin, I. (2025) *2025 UiPath Agentic AI Report - Preparing for the Agentic Era*, https://www.uipath.com/assets/downloads/agentic-ai-research-report. Accessed on 14 May 2025.

3 Tse, T. and Esposito, M. (2017) *Understanding How the Future Unfolds: Using DRIVE to Harness the Power of Today's Megatrends*. Austin, TX: Lioncrest Publishing.

4 Ghose, R., Bantanidis, S., Master, K., Shah, R. S., Chahal, S., Sharma, P. and Zhai, C. (2025) *Agentic AI: Finance & the 'Do It for Me' Economy*, https://www.citiwarrants.com/home/upload/citi_research/rsch_pdf_30305836.pdf. Accessed on 14 May 2025.

5 Purdy, M. (2024) "What is agentic AI, and how will it change work?," *Harvard Business Review*, https://hbr.org/2024/12/what-is-agentic-ai-and-how-will-it-change-work. Accessed on 19 December 2024.

6 Sung, S. (2024) *What Is Agentic AI?*, https://www.salesforce.com/agentforce/what-is-agentic-ai/?bc=OTH. Accessed on 28 December 2024.
7 Davenport, T. and Beck, J. (2001) *The Attention Economy: Understanding the New Currency of Business*. Boston: Harvard Business School Press.
8 Chaudhary, Y. and Penn, J. (2024) "Beware the intention economy: Collection and commodification of intent via large language models," *Harvard Data Science Review* (Special Issue 5), https://doi.org/10.1162/99608f92.21e6bbaa.
9 Harari, Y. N. (2024) *Nexus: A Brief History of Information Networks from the Stone Age to AI*. New York: Fern Press.
10 Abraham, A. (2024) "Computer says yes: how AI is changing our romantic lives," https://www.theguardian.com/technology/article/2024/jun/16/computer-says-yes-how-ai-is-changing-our-romantic-lives. Accessed on 26 February 2025.
11 Harari, Y. N. (2024) *Nexus: A Brief History of Information Networks from the Stone Age to AI*. New York: Fern Press.
12 Vigderman, A. and Turner, G. (2024) "The data big tech companies have on you," https://www.security.org/resources/data-tech-companies-have/. Accessed on 26 February 2025.
13 Lameiras, A. (2023) "One login to rule them all: Should you sign in with Google or Facebook on other websites?," https://www.welivesecurity.com/en/cybersecurity/one-login-rule-them-all-should-sign-in-google-facebook-other-websites/. Accessed on 26 February 2025.
14 Ramsey, T. (2025) "I'm a data expert: Here are 6 things I'd never do with my personal information," https://www.which.co.uk/news/article/im-a-data-expert-here-are-6-things-id-never-do-with-my-personal-information-aMHuv9C8EWH3. Accessed on 26 February 2025.
15 Morales, J. (2024) "Nvidia's future: A 50,000-person workforce enhanced by 100m AI agents," https://www.ccn.com/news/technology/nvidia-future-workforce-jensen-huang/. Accessed on 24 February 2025.
16 Ghose, R., Bantanidis, S., Master, K., Shah, R. S., Chahal, S., Sharma, P. and Zhai, C. (2025) *Agentic AI: Finance & the 'Do It for Me' Economy*, https://www.citiwarrants.com/home/upload/citi_research/rsch_pdf_30305836.pdf. Accessed on 14 May 2025.
17 Tse, T., Esposito, M. and Goh, D. (2022) "The comeback of traditional banks," https://blogs.lse.ac.uk/businessreview/2022/11/07/the-comeback-of-traditional-banks/. Accessed on 27 February 2025.
18 Davenport, T. H. (2022) "How legacy companies can pivot to a platform model," *Harvard Business Review*, https://hbr.org/2022/03/how-legacy-companies-can-pivot-to-a-platform-model. Accessed on 14 May 2025; Guillén, M. F. and Reddy, S. (2019) "How to turn a traditional business into a platform-based success," https://www.weforum.org/stories/2019/12/benefits-of-platform-business-model/. Accessed on 27 February 2025.
19 Locsin, M. (n.d.) "Platforms are powerful business models — but pitfalls await the unwary," https://www.publicissapient.com/insights/platforms-are-powerful-business-models. Accessed on 27 February 2025.

20 Rest of World (2021) "Gig workers are uncertain, scared, and barely scraping by," https://restofworld.org/2021/the-global-gig-workers/. Accessed on 14 May 2025; Wall, T. (2025) "Gig economy firms warned by UK government they may be operating illegally," https://www.theguardian.com/business/2025/jan/25/gig-economy-firms-warned-by-uk-government-they-may-be-operating-illegally. Accessed on 14 May 2025; Forde, C. (2024) "The future of gig work: addressing pay and conditions," https://business.leeds.ac.uk/research-ceric/dir-record/research-blog/2299/the-future-of-gig-work-addressing-pay-and-conditions. Accessed on 14 May 2025; Bartholomew, J. (2025) "'It's hard to survive': why UK private hire drivers are striking on Valentine's Day," https://www.theguardian.com/business/2025/feb/14/its-hard-to-survive-why-uk-private-hire-drivers-are-striking-on-valentines-day. Accessed on 27 February 2025.
21 World Economic Forum (2025) *Future of Jobs Report 2025*, https://reports.weforum.org/docs/WEF_Future_of_Jobs_Report_2025.pdf. Accessed on 14 May 2025.
22 Pichai, S. and Hassabis, D. (2024) "Our next-generation model: Gemini 1.5," https://blog.google/technology/ai/google-gemini-next-generation-model-february-2024/. Accessed on 6 March 2025; Kilpatrick, L., Mallick, S. B. and Kofman, R. (2024) "Gemini 1.5 Pro 2M context window, code execution capabilities, and Gemma 2 are available today," https://developers.googleblog.com/en/new-features-for-the-gemini-api-and-google-ai-studio/. Accessed on 6 March 2025.
23 Pop, L. M., Lorga, M. and Lurcov, R. (2022) "Body-esteem, self-esteem and loneliness among social media young users," *International Journal of Environmental Research and Public Health*, 19(9), Article 5064, https://doi.org/10.3390/ijerph19095064; Edmonds, R. (2018) "Anxiety, loneliness and fear of missing out: The impact of social media on young people's mental health," https://www.centreformentalhealth.org.uk/anxiety-loneliness-and-fear-missing-out-impact-social-media-young-peoples-mental-health/. Accessed on 6 March 2025; O'Day, E. B. and Heimberg, R. G. (2021) "Social media use, social anxiety, and loneliness: A systematic review," *Computers in Human Behavior Reports*, 3, Article 100070, https://doi.org/10.1016/j.chbr.2021.100070.
24 Wegmann, E., Müller, S. M., Turel, O. and Brand, M. (2020) "Interactions of impulsivity, general executive functions, and specific inhibitory control explain symptoms of social-networks-use disorder: An experimental study," *Scientific Reports*, 10, Article 3866, https://doi.org/10.1038/s41598-020-60819-4; Kossowska, M., Kłodkowski, P., Siewierska-Chmaj, A., Guinote, A., Kessels, U., Moyano, M. and Strömbäck, J. (2023) "Internet-based micro-identities as a driver of societal disintegration," *Humanities and Social Sciences Communications*, 10, Article 955, https://doi.org/10.1057/s41599-023-02441-z.
25 Wiggers, K. (2025) "Researchers open source Sky-T1, a 'reasoning' AI model that can be trained for less than $450," https://techcrunch.com/2025/01/11/researchers-open-source-sky-t1-a-reasoning-ai-model-that-can-be-trained-for-less-than-450/. Accessed on 6 March 2025.

26 Muennighoff, N., Yang, Z., Shi, W., Li, X. L., Fei-Fei, L., Hajishirzi, H., Zettlemoyer, L., Liang, P., Candès, E. and Hashimoto, T. (2025) "s1: Simple test-time scaling," *Arxiv.org* [Preprint], https://arxiv.org/pdf/2501.19393. Accessed on 6 March 2025.

27 *Economist Impact* (2025) "AI for social good: The transformative nature of AI in developing and emerging markets," https://impact.economist.com/i/ai-for-social-good-the-transformative-nature-of-ai-in-developing-and-emerging-markets-6RtNiVHWi7JzkVOr53D2nR. Accessed on 16 May 2025; *Economist Impact* (2024) "A quantum leap for all: UNGA's vision for a digital future," https://impact.economist.com/sustainability/resilience-and-adaptation/a-quantum-leap-for-all-ungas-vision-for-a-digital-future. Accessed on 16 May 2025.

CHAPTER 8

AI Unchecked

EVERY DAY, WE SEE AI becoming increasingly pervasive in our lives. Many of us now use GenAI to draft emails, although we may have to do so discreetly and secretly, without our employers being aware. However, this growing reliance on AI raises concerns about potential over-dependence.[1] A relevant historical parallel can be observed in the decline of memorisation skills, such as the decreased ability to recall phone numbers after the widespread adoption of mobile phones. As Nicholas Carr wrote in his book, we have allowed automation to diminish our skills and expertise.[2] With AI's expanding capabilities in both professional and personal spheres, we will increasingly delegate more essential tasks and decision-making processes to automated systems. Meanwhile, the lack of responsible governance in AI development and deployment poses significant risks. While AI offers substantial opportunities for societal advancement and problem-solving, its misuse, unintended consequences, or unregulated application can lead to profound challenges. One of the most pressing concerns is safeguarding data privacy and security within the AI landscape. In response, numerous commercial and governmental organisations have, particularly in recent years, developed ethical guidelines and regulatory frameworks to ensure the responsible development and application of AI technologies in real-world contexts. We cannot leave AI unchecked. This chapter examines the downsides of AI and the mitigation actions needed. We have discussed what AI can do for us. Now, we turn to what we must not allow AI to take over completely.

DOI: 10.1201/9781003559665-8

REGULATORY CHALLENGES IN AI GOVERNANCE

National governments frequently establish AI commissions to address emerging challenges in this rapidly evolving field. The European Union (EU) has been particularly active in this regard. In April 2019, the European Commission published the *Ethics Guidelines for Trustworthy Artificial Intelligence*, developed by a high-level expert group on AI. The guidelines outline a comprehensive framework for "trustworthy AI," grounded in fundamental rights and ethical principles that align with the core values of European institutions.[3] These principles include respect for human autonomy, dignity, democratic values, the rule of law, and justice. Building upon these foundational principles, the EU's expert group formulated seven key guidelines for AI.

- It is imperative that AI systems are subjected to human agency and oversight, acknowledging the need for human involvement in their operation and regulation;
- The technical robustness and safety of AI systems must be prioritised, emphasising the necessity for their reliability and security;
- Preserving privacy should be a fundamental consideration in developing and implementing AI systems and safeguarding individuals' personal information.
- AI systems should exhibit transparency, ensuring that individuals are informed when engaging with an artificial system, thereby promoting honesty and clarity in human-AI interactions;
- Promoting diversity, non-discrimination, and fairness should be integral to AI systems, fostering inclusivity and equality in their design and deployment;
- AI systems should be designed to serve the betterment of society and the environment, recognising their potential impact on societal and environmental well-being;
- The notion of accountability is crucial in AI, necessitating that AI systems are answerable for their actions and decisions, including external scrutiny and oversight.[4]

While good intentions drive all of these aspects, a critical question remains whether the EU will translate its ethical principles for AI into formal regulations, mirroring its approach to digital governance, as exemplified by the General Data Protection Regulation (GDPR), a many-headed beast of a law that took a decade to assemble. The regime is also about serious enforcement, at least in theory. It allows supervisory authorities to impose fines of as much as 4% of a company's yearly worldwide revenue. Implemented in 2016, the GDPR requires compliance for companies operating within the EU and has had significant global repercussions. For instance, Japan aligned its data privacy laws with European standards, and California enacted the California Consumer Privacy Act (CCPA) in 2018, with ongoing discussions regarding further harmonisation with the GDPR.[5] These regulatory alignments were partly driven by pursuing a GDPR "adequacy determination," which facilitates data transfers between Europe and these jurisdictions. However, due to its stringent data protection and transparency requirements, the GDPR has faced stiff opposition by potentially impeding AI innovation within European technology companies, contesting that the mandated human oversight of AI-driven decisions would substantially increase operational costs. Critics argue that the GDPR may hinder AI development in Europe without modifications, potentially redirecting investment towards regions with looser and more relaxed regulations, such as China and the United States. Beyond the EU, various governmental bodies and multilateral institutions have worked on AI ethics guidelines, often influenced by the EU's regulatory approach.[6] The Organization for Economic Co-operation and Development (OECD) provides a notable example, having published five complementary, value-based principles for responsible AI in May 2019.[7]

ALGORITHMIC BIAS AND ETHICAL CHALLENGES IN AI DECISION-MAKING

The discourse surrounding AI ethics remains highly dynamic and contentious, particularly regarding AI-driven decision-making processes that impact individuals based on sensitive attributes such as gender, socioeconomic status, sexual orientation, ethnicity, race, and religion. AI systems increasingly shape access to public and private resources and influence surveillance practices, employment screening, credit scoring, law enforcement, and judicial processes. These applications involve categorisation and evaluation, determining inclusion or exclusion, ultimately impacting individuals' life opportunities. With the benefits of hindsight, this is perhaps unavoidable. AI systems learn from the data they are trained on, and if that data reflects existing societal biases, the AI will inevitably inherit and perpetuate those biases.[8] This phenomenon can lead to discriminatory outcomes in various domains, including hiring, loan applications, and the criminal justice system. For example, an AI system trained on historical data that shows women are less likely to be promoted in a particular industry may unfairly disadvantage female candidates in future hiring decisions, even if they are equally or more qualified. This is the hard lesson that Amazon learned with its hiring algorithm.[9] This process perpetuates existing gender inequalities and hinders progress towards a more equitable society. A 2018 MIT Media Lab study found that facial recognition systems misidentified darker skinned women 34% of the time, compared to a near 0% error rate for lighter skinned men.[10] Google's image search algorithm demonstrated limitations in accurately identifying individuals from minority ethnic groups.[11] Moreover, AI systems don't just perpetuate; they also amplify existing biases. This phenomenon occurs because AI algorithms can identify and exploit subtle patterns in data that humans may not even be aware of. As a result, AI systems can make even more biased decisions than the humans who created them. For instance, an AI system used for risk assessment in criminal justice may assign higher risk scores to individuals from particular racial or ethnic groups, even if they have criminal histories similar to those of individuals from other groups. This process can lead to harsher sentencing and perpetuate systemic racism within the justice system.

Despite the lack of explicit intent to discriminate, these outcomes demonstrate how biases inherent in training data can influence algorithmic decisions. Indeed, Conway's Law applies to AI. The law states that in the absence of clear rules and instructions, the choices made by the team tend to reflect the implicit values of their group. Therefore, as long as beliefs, attitudes, behaviours, and hidden cognitive biases are firmly entrenched, Conway's Law will continue to prevail.[12] How the LLMs are trained can also perpetuate wrong ideas. The problem with the "tyranny of the majority" arises when most data sources mention an idea used to train LLMs. Although the concept is incorrect, it will always be the guiding principle—data volume rules. For instance, since 1994, Emma Rothschild has demolished the commonly misunderstood meaning of Adam Smith's invisible hand. Yet, OpenAI's Deep Research, made available in 2025, still repeats the old, wrong concept.[13]

POLICY RESPONSES TO ALGORITHMIC BIAS

Governments have increasingly sought to address concerns regarding algorithmic bias through legislative measures. In April 2019, US senators introduced the *Algorithmic Accountability Act*, which mandated that companies assess their AI algorithms and training data for biases and discriminatory outcomes.[14] Under this legislation, AI systems utilising sensitive personal data, such as race, gender, sexual orientation, religion, genetic and biometric attributes, and criminal history, would be classified as "high-risk" and subject to additional scrutiny. More recently, the *Algorithmic Accountability Act of 2023* expanded these provisions by requiring companies to evaluate the societal impacts of AI systems they develop, implement new transparency measures regarding AI usage, and empower consumers to make informed decisions when interacting with AI technologies. Despite these legislative efforts, the bill's ultimate fate remains uncertain, reflecting broader debates on the appropriate regulatory approach to AI governance.

POTENTIAL RISKS OF UNCHECKED AI

In September 2024, on the occasion of the *International Day of Democracy*, Secretary-General António Guterres reiterated the importance of upholding free speech, civil liberties, and the rule of law, as well as ensuring accountable institutions and protecting human rights. "Yet, these rights and values are under attack around the world. Freedoms are being eroded. Civic space is diminishing. Polarisation is intensifying. And mistrust is growing," he said, adding a plea: "It's crucial to ensure effective differences of AI at all levels, including internationally. AI must serve humanity equitably and safely."[15] The UN Secretary-General's warning highlights a critical concern about the unchecked development of AI. AI's capacity to generate highly realistic fake videos and audio recordings, known as deepfakes, poses a significant threat to democratic processes. These fabricated media can be used to spread disinformation, manipulate public opinion, and sow discord, potentially undermining trust in institutions and eroding the foundations of democracy. Imagine a deepfake video of a political leader making inflammatory remarks going viral before an election, or fabricated evidence used to discredit a key witness in a court case. The potential for AI to be weaponised in this way is a serious cause for alarm.

Furthermore, as AI algorithms can inadvertently amplify existing societal biases, hate speech and discriminatory content can be quickly spread.[16] If left unaddressed, these biases would likely keep exacerbating social divisions and fuelling extremism. AI-powered recommendation systems, for example, can create echo chambers and filter bubbles, reinforcing existing beliefs and limiting exposure to diverse perspectives. We already see the consequences: opinions have polarised, and finding common ground on critical issues has become significantly more challenging. The potential for AI to manipulate public discourse and undermine social cohesion is, therefore, a clear and present danger.

Autonomous Weapons

The prospect of weaponising AI-powered systems is a grave concern with far-reaching implications for global security. Autonomous weapons, often referred to as "killer robots," raise serious ethical questions about delegating life-or-death decisions to machines. These systems, programmed to identify and engage targets without human intervention, could malfunction or be hacked, leading to unintended casualties and the escalation of conflicts. Imagine a scenario where an autonomous weapon system misidentifies a civilian target or is reprogrammed by a malicious actor to attack friendly forces. The potential for catastrophic consequences is undeniable. Furthermore, developing autonomous weapons could destabilise international relations and fuel a new arms race. Over 30 countries have called for bans on autonomous weapons, recognising their potential for uncontrolled harm.[17] As nations compete to develop and deploy these systems, the risk of miscalculation and accidental conflict increases. The lack of human oversight in critical moments can lead to rapid escalation, with devastating consequences for both civilians and combatants. The potential for autonomous weapons to lower the threshold for the use of force and undermine international humanitarian law is a serious concern that demands urgent attention.

Economic Displacement

Due to skill mismatches, the transition to AI in the public and private sectors may leave many workers behind. The rapid advancement of automation and AI technologies has sparked widespread concern about the future of work and its potential impact on employment. In the previous chapters, we have discussed the vast range of economic and social opportunities that AI can offer. However, the rise of the machine also poses a substantial risk of job displacement on a colossal scale. The International Labour Organization has highlighted that the manufacturing, logistics, and retail industries are particularly vulnerable to job displacement driven by AI.[18] We have been warned that the massive unemployment could turn into a social crisis.[19] And this was way before the emergence of GenAI. A recent study of over 1.3 million freelance jobs online between 2021 and 2023 found that introducing ChatGPT and image-generating tools led to nearly immediate and steep decreases in posts for online gig workers across job types but more pronounced for automation-prone jobs.[20] As AI and automation take over tasks previously performed by humans, the demand for low-skilled labour may decline, applying downward pressure to wages. With fewer jobs kicking around for those with limited education and skills, there will inevitably be an increase in competition for automation-prone roles. At the same time, we will be seeing a proliferation of positions for the technology-astute as AI development charges speedily ahead. All of these would exacerbate income disparities and create a two-tiered workforce. Let's not forget that GenAI is effectively decentralising access to knowledge and creativity, empowering individuals without specialised training to develop professional-quality content. Now imagine the further impact on job markets—and the social implications—when AI agents become prominent, allowing a single professional or small team to expand their reach and influence in an unprecedented fashion dramatically.

Sure, the nature of jobs is going to change. However, the real difficulties lie in the need for continuous retraining and adaptation to a constantly evolving job market. Financial struggles will likely arise, particularly in supporting individuals who have lost their jobs while transitioning and acquiring new skills. Additionally, psychological difficulties will also emerge for these individuals.[21] Indeed, as AI agents stand ready to revolutionise individual productivity in the workplace, enabling greater output with less effort, we must consider the implications for those in junior positions and supporting functions. What future awaits professionals who traditionally filled entry-level roles? In this scenario, a growing segment of the population will struggle to find stable employment and economic security.

The New Digital Divide

What we are facing is no stranger to history. For centuries, technological revolutions have reshaped the workforce. Each new wave of innovation has caused seismic shifts in labour markets, from the spinning jenny displacing hand-weavers to assembly lines replacing skilled artisans. AI is no different, but the stakes today may be much higher. The rise of AI-native technologies and GenAI is not just automating tasks; it is reshaping the very nature of expertise and widening the skill—and not just the economic—gap, leading to a new digital divide. Conventional wisdom holds that automation disproportionately affects lower skilled routine jobs. However, GenAI complicates this narrative. As mentioned in an earlier chapter,

GenAI has demonstrated the ability to enhance the performance of workers with weaker skills.

There is an increasing amount of evidence showing how GenAI is helping those who are more skilled. For instance, more competent entrepreneurs could raise their profits by over 15% with the help of AI, while those less skilled saw their earnings decline. The distinction lay in how they utilised AI recommendations. Low achievers followed broad advice, such as ramping up advertising, whereas high achievers harnessed AI to pinpoint strategic solutions—such as securing alternative power sources during outages.[22] AI-powered materials discovery software demonstrated a significant difference in impact across researcher skill levels as well. The tool, which generated candidate materials based on specified properties, helped leading scientists nearly double their productivity. These top performers leveraged their deep subject expertise to effectively evaluate the AI's suggestions, distinguishing viable candidates from dead ends. However, the technology provided no productivity gains for researchers in the bottom third of performance, who found it challenging to determine which AI-generated suggestions were worth pursuing.[23] Better students are also found to be able to debate more effectively using GenAI.[24] The impact of AI tools on investment returns showed a clear divide based on investor expertise. While sophisticated investors leveraged the technology to boost their returns by nearly 10%, novice investors saw only modest gains of 2%. The key difference lay in how experienced investors could better interpret AI-derived insights from earnings calls, particularly when analysing nuanced financial metrics like R&D investments, share buybacks, and EBITDA (operating profit before depreciation and amortisation).[25] A conclusion that can be drawn here is that capitalising on AI-generated output requires more than technical literacy. It demands critical thinking, judgement, and domain expertise. As demonstrated in the study on financial decision-making, investors with a deeper understanding of these financial indicators can utilise AI analysis more effectively. Those who can navigate ambiguity, contextualise information, and make sophisticated decisions are poised to thrive in an AI-driven workplace. Those who cannot will struggle. In this sense, AI is not "democratising" knowledge and skills—it is tilting it even further in favour of the most skilled and adaptable.

So, it is not necessarily just how simple or complex or how narrowly scoped a task is. It is also about combining in-depth knowledge and expertise with technologies to achieve the most significant gains. Indeed, the latest research has found that LLMs' ability to tackle a task doesn't hinge so much on how intellectually demanding it is for humans or even the level of expertise required. Instead, it depends on how long the task takes a person to do and how "messy" or unstructured the process is. While executive assistant, travel agent, or bookkeeping clerk may sound like easy, entry-level roles, they remain (at least for now) out of reach for even the most advanced AI. Why? Because AI technologies struggle to keep track of multiple information streams, respond to a dynamic environment, work with unclear or changing goals and multi-task. Unlike neatly packaged coding problems or essay questions, the "messiness" of a task demands human-level flexibility and improvisation.[26] However, we cannot rest on our laurels. AI agents will eventually become significantly more capable of handling complex tasks.[27] Over time, we will have to run and upgrade our skills faster to stay in the same place. The new digital divide, therefore, is not just economic but also cognitive. Those who cultivate adaptability, curiosity, and deep expertise will harness AI to amplify their capabilities. Those who do not will be left behind. This is the "K-shaped" development our friend Kary Bheemaiah has described: the capable few accelerate and rise ahead, while others fall into stagnation and behind.[28] This means it is unlikely that we will all become "CEOs of AI agents": the most talented and adaptable individuals will become the best AI CEOs, while the rest risk becoming mere spectators in the unfolding revolution.

Misinformation and Deepfakes

AI-generated content, such as deepfakes, can spread misinformation, disrupt elections, or damage reputations. The ability of AI to generate incredibly realistic but entirely fabricated content, like deepfakes, poses a significant threat to truth and trust. In 2019, a deepfake video of Facebook's CEO Mark Zuckerberg, created to demonstrate AI's potential misuse, raised awareness about the difficulty of detecting manipulated content.[29] Deepfake technology has been used for fraud, as seen in 2019 when a CEO was tricked into transferring $243,000 after a scammer used AI to mimic his boss's voice.[30] A Hong Kong employee at a British engineering giant got duped by a deceiving troupe: deepfake videos of his colleagues, including the finance chief, on a convincing video call. What is the price tag for this digital masquerade? $25 million straight from the company's coffers.[31] A French woman fell victim to an elaborate romance scam after being deceived by scammers using AI-generated images and videos to impersonate actor Brad Pitt. The fraudsters cultivated a fake romantic relationship with the victim over several months, eventually convincing her to part company with €830,000.[32] Unsurprisingly, half of all fraud detected today is believed to have incorporated some form of AI.[33] AI-powered phishing attacks, for example, have become significantly more advanced. Instead of generic and easily detectable emails, AI can generate persuasive fake emails tailored to specific individuals. These emails can mimic the language, style, and even personal details of trusted contacts, making them virtually indistinguishable from legitimate correspondence. Deepfakes can convincingly portray individuals saying or doing things they never did, potentially spreading misinformation on a massive scale. This phenomenon can have serious consequences, particularly in the context of elections, where manipulated videos could be used to smear candidates, influence voters, or even incite violence. Imagine a deepfake video circulating on social media that falsely depicts a candidate making offensive remarks or engaging in illegal activity. Such disinformation could quickly spread, influencing public opinion and potentially disrupting the democratic process.

Beyond the political realm, AI-generated content can also damage reputations and harm individuals. Deepfakes can be weaponised to create compromising or embarrassing situations, leading to social ostracism, job loss, or even threats of violence. This potential raises serious concerns about privacy, safety, and the risk of malicious actors exploiting AI for personal gain or revenge. The ease with which such content can be created and disseminated makes it a powerful tool for manipulation and abuse, with potentially devastating consequences for individuals and society. The risk posed by deepfakes is not just about people believing falsehoods; it also leads to the very notion of truth declining in value. This raises the question of how to address this. Some will wish them to be outlawed; others will see them as legitimate or helpful forms of free expression. Currently, governments have delegated this issue to technology companies. So, here is another question: Are the values held by these companies aligned with that social good?

AI Suppliers' Accountability

During 2016–2017, Myanmar's military forces and Buddhist extremist groups conducted systematic ethnic cleansing operations targeting the Rohingya population. The campaign was driven by deep-seated animosity towards the Rohingya community as a whole. This hatred was intensified through widespread anti-Rohingya propaganda, which found a particularly effective distribution channel through Facebook. By 2016, Facebook had become the primary news source for millions in Myanmar and the country's dominant platform for political organisation and mobilisation.[34] Its parent, Meta, has later been found to have substantially and systematically contributed to adverse human rights impacts suffered by the Rohingya and has a responsibility to provide survivors with an adequate remedy.[35] Yet, the social media company's response to most alleged algorithmic harm has primarily been one of deflection. Rather than acknowledging the inherent problems with their engagement-driven algorithms, major platforms like Facebook, YouTube, and TikTok have attempted to place the burden primarily on their users, suggesting their only failing was inadequate content moderation rather than algorithmic priorities. These companies often try to deflect criticism of their algorithmic systems by attributing it to "human nature," questioning why users create and share harmful content on their platforms in the first place. This defence overlooks a crucial reality: while human beings are multi-faceted creatures capable of expressing a wide range of emotions and moral values, these algorithms reduce human experience to a single metric: engagement. This reductive approach to human behaviour has given rise to a novel form of social organisation that differs markedly from traditional human interaction. Prioritising engagement above all else has resulted in amplifying misinformation and false narratives.[36]

Can we trust that technology giants and AI suppliers will produce responsible AI or at least acknowledge their responsibility when an AI fails? As AI evolves, a few technology giants have established effective monopolies over the essential building blocks of AI development: vast computing resources, extensive datasets, and specialised technical knowledge, not to mention LLMs, which are poised to become the infrastructure for much of the future AI development. This dominance has compelled smaller companies to enter into asymmetrical partnerships with, or undergo acquisitions by, larger entities to access these critical resources. Prominent examples include Google's acquisition of DeepMind and Microsoft's $13 billion "alliance" with OpenAI. The market power of these giants extends beyond AI, encompassing critical infrastructure such as search engines, cloud computing platforms, and web browsers. This existing dominance allows them to create ecosystems that guide users towards their proprietary AI models and services. As more users engage with and contribute data to these dominant AI platforms, network effects and economies of scale further amplify the advantages the giant AI suppliers enjoy. With all this power, expecting these giants to accept responsibility for AI-induced problems would be challenging.[37] Lately, it has become apparent that technology giants don't just follow where the money is—they follow where political—and subsequently economic—advantages can be gained. Meta's latest decision to dispense with the need for fact verification is the case in point. The company believes these fact-checkers had become "too politically biased … destroying more trust than they've created, especially in the US."[38] All of these put AI suppliers' accountability in question.

Loss of Human Autonomy

Automation has a way of eroding skills over time. When Air France Flight 447 plunged into the Atlantic in 2009, investigators found that the pilots had failed to respond correctly to a loss of airspeed data. The reason? Decades of reliance on automated flight systems had dulled their ability to recover manually from stall conditions.[39] Similarly, the so-called "Google Effect" has made us more dependent on external knowledge repositories, weakening our ability to retain information.[40] AI will likely amplify this trend. The more we outsource writing, analysis, and decision-making to machines, the greater our risk of losing the ability to think critically and independently. This effect is already being observed in education. While GenAI can be a powerful learning tool, researchers have found that students who rely heavily on AI-generated responses tend to perform worse on exams. Intriguingly, the negative impact is most pronounced among students with high learning potential. By allowing AI to do the heavy lifting for them, those individuals who might have otherwise excelled through deep engagement and struggle could have short-circuited their learning processes.[41]

We are not only losing our autonomy in terms of skills, but we are also relinquishing our ability to make informed decisions in the AI-native era.

Recall that with the advancement of AI, the technology would be increasingly capable of anticipating our desires and preferences. `Rather than merely presenting options, these AI-driven systems can actively shape our choices, often flying under our radar of awareness. This could become a particularly acute problem in an AI-native setting, where AI agents are designed to proactively achieve goals on our behalf and make decisions to fulfil our anticipated desires. This gradual erosion of "self-governance" can have profound consequences, diminishing our sense of agency and control over our lives. As we increasingly rely on these systems to guide our decisions, we risk becoming passive recipients of algorithmic influence, losing the ability to assess changes in our surrounding landscape and act independently critically, arguably essential human skills for thriving in an AI-native world.

Compelling evidence for a loss of such autonomy can be seen in how social media algorithms have polarised content. Optimised for engagement rather than protecting social welfare, these algorithms often prioritise sensational and divisive material, which tends to capture attention and generate more interaction. This prioritisation has a cascading effect, creating echo chambers where users are primarily exposed to information that reinforces their biases, further polarising opinions and hindering constructive dialogue. The documentary *The Social Dilemma* illustrates how AI-driven platforms exploit psychological vulnerabilities to maximise user engagement, often at the expense of users' mental well-being.[42] By leveraging techniques like personalised recommendations and targeted advertising, these platforms can subtly manipulate users' emotions and beliefs, leading to addiction, anxiety, and a distorted perception of reality. The "filter bubble" concept highlights how algorithmic curation on social media creates echo chambers, reinforcing users' beliefs by presenting them with content that aligns with their preferences.[43] These algorithms, driven by statistical learning models, categorise users into rigid groups based on their interactions, shaping their digital experience and, in extreme cases, promoting misinformation and conspiracy theories. Today, a parallel phenomenon is emerging: the "generative bubble."[44] Whereas filter bubbles are created by algorithms that control what users see, generative bubbles arise from how users interact with GenAI tools. The quality and diversity of AI-generated content depend on the user's ability to craft precise prompts. Individuals with limited experience, knowledge, or a reluctance to experiment may receive narrow, repetitive, or even misleading outputs. Unlike the filter bubble, where external algorithms dictate content exposure, the generative bubble is a self-imposed limitation shaped by the user's engagement style.

This ultimately introduces a new form of bias—adoption bias—where factors such as education, cultural background, and cognitive habits influence how effectively people utilise GenAI. Even highly educated users can fall into intellectual ruts, structuring prompts to reinforce their existing viewpoints rather than expand their understanding. These biases, shaped by history, institutions, and social structures, mean that AI adoption is never neutral—it reflects the political, economic, and cultural forces and beliefs of its time. Indeed, traditional AI has seemingly diminished our intellectual autonomy. One study has demonstrated that algorithms designed to nudge people towards specific content could significantly influence their opinions.[45] By subtly manipulating the information presented to users, these algorithms can effectively steer their beliefs and attitudes, even on complex and nuanced issues. This phenomenon underscores the influence of persuasive AI on shaping our understanding of the world, raising concerns about the potential for manipulation and the erosion of independent thought. When algorithms can subtly influence our opinions, the notion of free and informed consent becomes questionable.

As AI agents advance, they increasingly handle cognitive tasks once exclusive to humans—from observation and analysis to judgement and decision-making. While humans transition towards oversight and validation roles, this shift in reality goes beyond simple replacement. This is because algorithmic systems may narrow our cognitive scope rather than expanding human potential, leading us to trade in nuanced expertise for standardised mechanical responses. Although automation is often widely praised as a benefit, we frequently fall into what could be termed the "substitution fallacy." On the surface, machines seamlessly replace human labour to make productivity gains. Yet, automation fundamentally transforms the nature of work and our fundamental abilities. When we automate a task, we don't just transfer it from human to machine—we alter its essential character unanticipatedly. The fact is that when we tackle a task with our minds and hands, our brains light up with activity different from when we lean on computers as crutches. Consider what happens as AI increasingly relegates us to passive observers: we stop wrestling with problems, stop feeling our way through challenges, and stop building those neural pathways that come from hands-on experience. It is like learning to play basketball by watching games from the bench instead of getting out on the court. The more we outsource our thinking to AI, the more we rob ourselves of that hard-won, practical wisdom that only comes from doing. This is not just about losing skills but about losing our capacity to understand how things work intensely, intuitively, and truly.

Hacking and Security Threats

The increasing reliance on AI systems presents a dual threat to cybersecurity. AI systems are vulnerable to cyberattacks; malicious actors can also use them to execute sophisticated hacks. Such double trouble has potential consequences ranging from data breaches and financial losses to compromised safety systems and physical harm. As AI becomes more integrated into critical infrastructure and everyday technologies, the stakes associated with these threats become increasingly high. One significant vulnerability of AI systems is their susceptibility to adversarial attacks. These attacks involve subtly manipulating input data, such as images or text, in ways imperceptible to humans but can completely fool AI systems. In 2020, researchers demonstrated the effectiveness of these attacks by showing how they could trick AI systems into misclassifying images.[46] This potential has profound implications for safety-critical applications, such as self-driving cars, where a misclassified stop sign could lead to a serious accident, or security systems, where a misidentified individual could gain unauthorised access. The ease with which these attacks can be carried out highlights the need for robust defences and continuous improvement in the security of AI systems.

MITIGATING THE RISKS

Despite the inherent dangers, AI holds immense potential to transform and strengthen democratic systems positively. Rather than being solely a threat, AI can be a powerful tool for promoting full and active public participation, enhancing equality, and significantly contributing to human development. By automating tedious tasks, analysing vast amounts of data, and facilitating communication, AI can empower citizens, improve governance, and create more inclusive and responsive democratic processes. Such improvement, however, relies on our ability to harness AI responsibly and ethically, mitigating risks while maximising benefits. As the UN Secretary-General highlighted, AI can be crucial in boosting education on democratic processes.[47] AI-powered platforms can provide citizens with accessible and engaging information about government policies, electoral processes, and civic rights. Furthermore, AI can help shape more inclusive civic spaces where individuals have a meaningful voice in decisions and can hold decision-makers accountable. For instance, AI-driven tools can analyse public sentiment, identify emerging issues, and facilitate dialogue between citizens and their representatives. This potential can foster more responsive and representative governance, strengthening the bond between the public and their elected officials. While the potential benefits are significant, it is essential to recognise and address the risks associated with AI. A multifaceted approach encompassing regulation, transparency, and ethical AI design is necessary for this purpose.[48] Governments and international organisations must establish clear ethical guidelines and enforce laws governing the development and deployment of AI. Transparency is paramount; developers must prioritise explainable AI, ensuring we understand how these systems make decisions. Such transparency is crucial for establishing trust and preventing AI from being exploited in ways that undermine democratic values. Furthermore, ethical AI design is critical, necessitating the training of AI systems with diverse, unbiased datasets and prioritising accountability in their development and use.

Given the imminent impact of AI on the workforce, governments, businesses, and educational institutions must collaborate to invest in education and training programmes that prepare workers for the jobs of the future. These efforts include promoting lifelong learning, providing affordable education and skills development opportunities, and supporting workers as they transition to new careers. Furthermore, it is crucial to consider policies that ensure a fair distribution of the benefits of AI and automation, such as universal basic income or other social safety nets, to mitigate the potential for increased economic inequality.

Another significant challenge stems from AI-generated content, particularly deepfakes. Addressing this requires a multi-pronged approach. Technology companies must develop tools and technologies to detect and flag deepfakes, while media literacy initiatives can empower individuals to evaluate information and critically identify potential manipulation. Furthermore, legal frameworks may be necessary to hold creators and distributors of malicious deepfakes accountable for the harm they cause. It is crucial to balance freedom of expression and the need to protect individuals and society from the potential harms of AI-generated disinformation. Bias in AI systems is yet another area requiring focused attention. Addressing this challenge requires a concerted effort to ensure that AI systems are trained on diverse and representative datasets. This effort includes actively collecting data from under-represented groups and mitigating biases in existing datasets. Furthermore, it is crucial to develop AI algorithms that are transparent and accountable, allowing for human oversight and intervention to prevent discriminatory outcomes. By taking proactive steps to address bias in AI, we can harness its potential for good while mitigating its potential to perpetuate and amplify societal inequalities.

The use of AI in military applications presents another critical concern. The international community must act decisively to prevent the unchecked proliferation of autonomous weapons. This effort requires establishing clear ethical guidelines and regulations for developing and deploying AI in military applications. It is essential to ensure that human control and accountability remain central to any use of force and that AI systems are designed and used in a manner that respects international humanitarian law and human rights. The future of warfare and global security hinges on our ability to address these challenges responsibly and ethically. We may soon need an AI equivalent of the Nuclear Non-Proliferation Treaty.

The broader ethical implications of AI development and deployment necessitate a comprehensive strategy. Governments, AI companies of all sizes, and civil society organisations need to work together to develop ethical guidelines and regulations for the responsible development and deployment of AI.[49] This collaboration includes promoting transparency and accountability in AI systems, investing in media literacy and critical thinking skills, and fostering a culture of responsible technology use. It is crucial to ensure that AI is used to enhance democratic values and promote social good rather than being exploited to undermine them. The future of democracy may depend on our ability to harness the power of AI while mitigating its potential risks. To address this, we need greater transparency in how these systems operate so individuals can understand how they are being influenced.

Education and critical thinking skills are essential for navigating the complex information landscape and resisting manipulation. Furthermore, policymakers and technology companies must prioritise ethical considerations in designing and deploying AI systems, ensuring that they serve humanity rather than the other way around. By fostering awareness, promoting critical thinking, and demanding ethical AI development, we can reclaim our agency in the age of intelligent machines and safeguard our fundamental freedoms.

As individuals, we must take action against AI-reinforced echo chambers and generative bubbles by being able to see beyond the screens, reading a variety of topics both online and offline, socialising and continuously interrogating our existing beliefs and views. Unfortunately, this could be a lost cause, considering how many people today struggle to stay away from their mobile phones for long. A recent survey has found that people in the United States check their phones an average of 205 times a day. Nearly 90% of respondents check their phone within the first 10 minutes of waking up, with around 75% stating that they check their phone while in the bathroom. About 57% acknowledged they were addicted to the devices.[50] Finally, the security of AI systems themselves is paramount. Addressing these dual threats requires a multifaceted approach. Researchers must continue to develop robust defences against adversarial attacks and improve the security of AI systems. Furthermore, cybersecurity professionals must stay ahead of the curve by understanding how AI can be weaponised and developing strategies to counter these advanced attacks. These efforts include educating users about the risks of AI-powered phishing and other social engineering tactics. Finally, policymakers must consider the security implications of AI and develop regulations that promote the responsible development and deployment of these technologies. We can only mitigate the risks associated with AI in cybersecurity and ensure a safer digital future through a concerted and collaborative effort.

By utilising AI for good governance, countries can create more transparent and accountable systems that empower citizens to engage more effectively in democratic processes. However, realising this vision requires effective governance of AI at all levels, including internationally. Global cooperation is essential to ensure that AI is developed and used to benefit humanity rather than exacerbating existing inequalities or undermining democratic principles.[51] Stakeholders should share best practices, establish common standards, and foster dialogue between governments, researchers, and the public. Only through a concerted and collaborative effort can we unlock AI's full potential for democratic enhancement and build a future where technology strengthens rather than undermines our democratic values.

NOTES

1 Esposito, Mark, Tse, Terence and Saheb, Tahereh Sonia (2023) "Can businesses help build trustworthy and accurate generative AI?" *World Economic Forum*, https://www.weforum.org/stories/2023/03/generative-ai-accuracy-trust-business/. Accessed on 12 February 2025.

2 Carr, Nicolas (2015) *The Glass Cage: Who Needs Humans Anyway?* London: Vintage.

3 European Commission, Directorate-General for Communications Networks, Content and Technology (2019) *Ethics Guidelines for Trustworthy AI*, https://data.europa.eu/doi/10.2759/346720. Accessed on 12 February 2025.

4 European Commission, Directorate-General for Communications Networks, Content and Technology (2019) *Ethics Guidelines for Trustworthy AI*, https://data.europa.eu/doi/10.2759/346720. Accessed on 12 February 2025.

5 Gribakov, Andrei (2019) "Road to adequacy: Can California apply under the GDPR?," *Lawfare*, April 22, https://www.lawfaremedia.org/article/road-adequacy-can-california-apply-under-gdpr. Accessed on 12 February 2025.

6 Christou, Giorge, Meyer, Trisha and Fanni, Rosanna (2025) "The European Union: Assessing global leadership through actorness in artificial intelligence," *Journal of European Integration*, 47(3), pp. 383–401

7 OECD.AI (2024) *OECD AI Principles Uverview*, https://oecd.ai/en/ai-principles. Accessed on 12 February 2025.
8 Esposito, Mark, Entsminger, Josh and Tse, Terence (2024) "The threat of persuasive AI," *Project Syndicate*, January 3, https://www.project-syndicate.org/commentary/persuasive-ai-poses-manipulation-disinformation-threats-by-mark-esposito-et-al-2024-01. Accessed on 12 February 2025.
9 Dastin, Jeffrey (2018) "Insight - Amazon scraps secret AI recruiting tool that showed bias against women," *Reuters*, October 11, https://www.reuters.com/article/world/insight-amazon-scraps-secret-ai-recruiting-tool-that-showed-bias-against-women-idUSKCN1MK0AG/. Accessed on 12 February 2025.
10 Hardesty, Larry (2018) "Study finds gender and skin-type bias in commercial artificial-intelligence systems," *MIT News Office*, February 11, https://news.mit.edu/2018/study-finds-gender-skin-type-bias-artificial-intelligence-systems-0212. Accessed on 12 February 2025.
11 Kayser-Bril, Nicolas (2020) "Google apologizes after its Vision AI produced racist results," *Algorithm Watch*, April 7, https://algorithmwatch.org/en/google-vision-racism/. Accessed on 12 February 2025.
12 Webb, Amy (2019) *The Big Nine: How the Tech Titans & Their Thinking Machines Could Warp Humanity*. New York: Public Affairs.
13 *The Economist* (2025) "The danger of relying on OpenAI's Deep Research", February 13, https://www.economist.com/finance-and-economics/2025/02/13/the-danger-of-relying-on-openais-deep-research. Accessed on 21 February 2025.
14 Williams, A. (2023) "What could horizontal AI legislation look like in the US? Exploring the US Algorithmic Accountability Act," https://www.holisticai.com/blog/us-algorithmic-accountability-act. Accessed 12 February 2025.
15 United Nations (2024) "Secretary-General's message on the International Day of Democracy," https://www.un.org/sg/en/content/sg/statement/ 2024-09-15/secretary-generals-message-the-international-day-of-democracy-scroll-down-for-french-version. Accessed on 12 February 2025.
16 Entsminger, Josh, Esposito, Mark, Tse, Terence and Jean, Aurelie (2023) "The dark side of generative AI: Automating inequality by design," *CMR Insights*, June 23, https://cmr.berkeley.edu/2023/06/the-dark-side-of-generative-ai-automating-inequality-by-design/. Accessed on 12 February 2025.
17 Human Rights Watch (2020) "Stopping killer robots - Country positions on banning fully autonomous weapons and retaining human control," August 10, https://www.hrw.org/report/2020/08/10/stopping-killer-robots/country-positions-banning-fully-autonomous-weapons-and. Accessed on 12 February 2025.
18 Chang, Jae-Hee, Rynhart, Gary and Huynh, Phu (2016) *ASEAN in Transformation – The Future of Jobs at Risk of Automation*. International Labour Organization, Bureau for Employers' Activities, Working Paper No. 9.
19 Ford, Martin (2016) *The Rise of the Robots: Technology and the Rise of Mass Unemployment*. London: Oneworld.

20 Demirci, Ozge, Hannane, Jonas and Zhu, Xinrong (2025) "Who is AI replacing? The impact of generative AI on online freelancing platforms," *Management Science*. https://doi.org/10.1287/mnsc.2024.05420
21 Harari, Yuval Noah (2024) *Nexus: A Brief History of Information Networks from the Stone Age to AI*. New York: Fern Press.
22 Otis, Nicholas, Clarke, Rowan, Delecourt, Solène, Holtz, David and Koning, Rembrand (2024) "The uneven impact of generative AI on entrepreneurial performance," *Social Science Research Network*, February 29, https://papers.ssrn.com/sol3/papers.cfm?abstract_id=4671369. Accessed on 21 February 2025.
23 Toner-Rodgers, Aidan (2024) "Artificial intelligence, scientific discovery, and product innovation," Arxiv, December 21, https://arxiv.org/abs/2412.17866. Accessed on 21 February 2025.
24 Roldan-Mones, Antonio (2024) "When GenAI increases inequality: Evidence from a university debating competition," *ESADE Working Paper*, August 26.
25 Kim, Alex G., Kim, David S., Muhn, Maximilian, Nikolaev, Valeri V. and So, Eric C. (2024) "AI, investment decisions, and inequality," *Becker Friedman Institute for Economics Working Paper*, December, 2025-02.
26 Barnes, Elizabeth, Becker, Joel, Bloom, Ryan, Broadley, Thomas, Chan, Lawrence, Deng, Amy, Du, Haoxing, Garcia, Katharyn, Goodrich, Brian, Harold Miles, Luke, Hasin, Max, Jawhar, Sami, Jurkovic, Nikola, Kinniment, Megan, Kwa, Thomas, Lin, Tao, Nix, Seraphina, Parikh, Neev, Rein, David, Sato, Lucas Jun Koba, Von Arx, Sydney, West, Ben, Wijk, Hjalmar and Ziegler, Daniel M. (2025) "Measuring AI ability to complete long tasks," *arxiv.org*, https://arxiv.org/pdf/2503.14499#page=14. Accessed on 2 April 2025.
27 Burn-Murdock, John (2025) "Why hasn't AI taken your job yet?," *Financial Times*, March 28, https://www.ft.com/content/471b5eba-2a71-4650-a019-e8d4065b78a0. Accessed on 2 April 2025.
28 Bheemaiah, Kary (2020) "New Normal 2.0: Tech & K-Shaped recovery," September 8, https://www.linkedin.com/pulse/new-normal-20-tech-k-shaped-recovery-kary-bheemaiah/. Accessed on 19 February 2025.
29 Metz, R. and O'Sullivan, D. (2019) "A deepfake video of Mark Zuckerberg presents a new challenge for Facebook," https://edition.cnn.com/2019/06/11/tech/zuckerberg-deepfake/index.html. Accessed 14 February 2025.
30 Sangfor Technologies (2024) "Fight against the rise of deepfake scams with AI and biometrics," https://www.sangfor.com/blog/cybersecurity/fight-against-deepfake-scams-with-ai-and-biometrics. Accessed 12 February 2025.
31 *The Economist* (2025) "The vast and sophisticated global enterprise that is Scam Inc", February 6, https://www.economist.com/leaders/2025/02/06/the-vast-and-sophisticated-global-enterprise-that-is-scam-inc. Accessed on 19 February 2025.
32 Gozzi, Laura (2025) "AI Brad Pitt dupes French woman out of €830,000", *BBC News*, January 15, https://www.bbc.co.uk/news/articles/ckgnz8rw1xgo. Accessed on 19 February 2025.

33 Imperva (2024) *Bad Bot Report*, April 16, https://www.imperva.com/resources/resource-library/reports/2024-bad-bot-report/. Accessed on 2 April 2025.

34 Thant, Myint-U (2021) *The Hidden History of Burma: Race, Capitalism, and the Crisis of Democracy in the 21st Century*. New York: W.W. Norton & Company.

35 Amnesty International (2022) *The Social Atrocity Meta and the Right to Remedy for the Rohingya*, downloadable on https://www.amnesty.org/en/documents/asa16/5933/2022/en/.

36 Murgia, Madhumita (2025) *Code Dependent: How AI Is Changing Our Lives*. London: Picador.

37 Riekeles, Georg and von Thun, Max (2023) "Rishi Sunak's AI plan has no teeth – and once again, big tech is ready to exploit that," *The Guardian*, November 16, https://www.theguardian.com/commentisfree/2023/nov/16/rishi-sunak-ai-plan-big-tech-control-protect. Accessed on 21 February 2025.

38 Duffy, Clare (2025) "Meta is getting rid of fact checkers. Zuckerberg acknowledged more harmful content will appear on the platforms now," *CNN*, January 7, https://edition.cnn.com/2025/01/07/tech/meta-censorship-moderation/. Accessed on 6 March 2025.

39 Carr, Nicolas (2016) *The Glass Cage: Who Needs Humans Anyway*. London: Vintage.

40 Sparrow, Betsey, Liu, Jenny and Wegner, Daniel M. (2011). "Google effects on memory: Cognitive consequences of having information at our fingertips," *Science*, 333(6043), 476–78.

41 Wecks, Janik Ole, Voshaar, Johannes, Plate, Benedikt J., Zimmermann, Jochen and Zimmermann, Jochen (2024) "Generative AI usage and exam performance," *SSRN*, November24.

42 Seibert, Jeff (2020) "The mechanics and psychology behind the social dilemma," *Medium*, March 13, https://medium.com/swlh/the-mechanics-and-psychology-behind-the-social-dilemma-719d618aa8ce. Accessed on 12 February 2025.

43 Pariser, Eli (2012) *The Filter Bubble: What the Internet Is Hiding from You*. London: Penguin.

44 Jean, Aurelie, Sibout, Guillaume, Esposito, Mark and Tse, Terence (2025) "Bolla Generativa: come la genAI sta cambiando il nostro modo di vedere il mondo," *MIT Technology Review*, February 12, https://www.technologyreview.it/bolla-generativa-come-la-genai-sta-cambiando-il-nostro-modo-di-vedere-il-mondo/. Accessed on 21 February 2025.

45 Jesse, Mathias and Jannach, Dietmar (2021) "Digital nudging with recommender systems: Survey and future directions", *Computers in Human Behavior Reports*, 3, 1000–52.

46 Povolny, Steve (2020) "Model hacking ADAS to pave safer roads for autonomous vehicles," *McAfee*, February 12, https://www.mcafee.com/blogs/other-blogs/mcafee-labs/model-hacking-adas-to-pave-safer-roads-for-autonomous-vehicles/. Accessed on 12 February 2025.

47 United Nations (2024) "Secretary-General's message on the International Day of Democracy," https://www.un.org/sg/en/content/sg/statement/2024-09-15/secretary-generals-message-the-international-day-of-democracy-scroll-down-for-french-version. Accessed on 12 February 2025.
48 United Nations (2024) "Secretary-General's message on the International Day of Democracy," https://www.un.org/sg/en/content/sg/statement/2024-09-15/secretary-generals-message-the-international-day-of-democracy-scroll-down-for-french-version. Accessed on 12 February 2025.
49 Esposito, Mark and Tse, Terence (2024). "Mitigating the risks of generative AI in government through algorithmic governance," *Social Science Research Network*, http://dx.doi.org/10.2139/ssrn.4811924. Accessed on 12 February 2025.
50 Wheelwright, Trevor (2025) "Cell Phone Usage Stats 2025: Americans check their phones 205 times a day," *Reviews.org*, January 1, https://www.reviews.org/mobile/cell-phone-addiction/. Accessed on 21 February 2025.
51 Ginsburg, Robert (2024) "Global governance of artificial intelligence and the Telegraph," *Forbes*, December 12, https://www.forbes.com/sites/robertginsburg/2024/12/18/ai-governance-and-the-telegraph-revolution/. Accessed on 12 February 2025.

CHAPTER 9

Conclusion

After dedicating these pages to exploring potential futures, sharing informed perspectives, and analysing the trajectory of AI's progress, we arrive at perhaps the most candid conclusion one can offer in any discourse on artificial intelligence: the precise path ahead remains fundamentally unknowable. We have explored AI's historical evolution, meticulously examined its current capabilities, and envisioned a future where AI is as pervasive as electricity. Nevertheless, despite this extensive analysis and detailed consideration of potential AI-driven scenarios, attempting to predict AI's exact course is akin to a meteorologist forecasting the precise landing spot of a single raindrop in next month's storm—we would be lying if we said we knew.

This inherent unpredictability extends even to those deeply immersed in AI development. While numerous experts offer confident pronouncements about AI's future, a healthy scepticism is warranted. History is replete with instances where AI's evolution has defied expectations. Indeed, even the most brilliant minds in AI research—the very architects of these technologies—frequently find themselves surprised by the emergent behaviours of their creations.

THE KNOWN UNKNOWNS OF AI

Despite DeepMind's reputation for pioneering AI research, the company reportedly underestimated the importance of generative models. According to insiders, this oversight may have stemmed from Generative AI (GenAI) not aligning with CEO Demis Hassabis's artificial general intelligence vision or the company's core reinforcement learning focus.

DOI: 10.1201/9781003559665-9

Regardless of the underlying reasons, this strategic blind spot resulted in DeepMind losing ground in what would become one of AI's most transformative domains.[1] Similarly revealing is the candid admission from Sam Altman, the founder and CEO of OpenAI. Despite leading the organisation that created ChatGPT, Altman has acknowledged that he did not anticipate the direction his company—and the underlying technology—would take. "We started off just thinking we were going to be a research lab and having no idea about how this technology was going to go," said Altman. "Because it was only seven or eight years ago, it's hard to go back and really remember what it was like then, but this is before language models were a big deal. This was before we had any idea about an API or selling access to a chatbot. It was before we had any idea we were going to productise at all. So we're like, 'We're just going to try to do research and we don't really know what we're going to do with that.' I think with many fundamentally new things, you start fumbling through the dark and you make some assumptions, most of which turned out to be wrong."[2]

Indeed, history has repeatedly demonstrated the limitations of human foresight.[3] While this reflects a general constraint in our ability to predict future events, the challenge in forecasting AI's trajectory extends beyond these typical forecasting difficulties. Human intuition often relies on extrapolating from existing trends. However, unlike phenomena such as climate change or the impact of ageing demographics, where underlying mechanisms, though complex, are relatively stable, the difficulty in predicting AI developments is significantly amplified by their fundamental and often unpredictable nature. AI's very building blocks and potential applications are in constant flux, rendering simple extrapolation an unreliable tool for strategic planning.

MOVE 37

In March 2016, AlphaGo, an AI developed by DeepMind, faced off against Lee Sedol, a world champion in the game of Go, in South Korea. Despite expectations that Sedol would win, AlphaGo emerged victorious in the first game. A key moment occurred during the second game with Move 37, which has since become a landmark in the history of both AI and Go. This move makes no sense in humans' eyes (and minds), leading commentators to believe AlphaGo had made a grave mistake. However, this seemingly erroneous move proved pivotal in AlphaGo's victory, demonstrating the AI's capacity to uncover novel strategies that had eluded human players for millennia. Effectively, the AI system discovered and explored new areas of Go that human minds had never considered venturing into. AlphaGo eventually went on to win the match 4-1. Later iterations, like AlphaZero, learned independently by playing against itself millions of times, surpassing human knowledge within a day.

Move 37 is emblematic of the unfathomability of AI.[4] AI's increasing complexity and opacity have made it difficult or impossible for humans to understand or explain fully. Even after AlphaGo's success, the creator team could not explain the reasoning behind Move 37. This mystery reflects a broader trend where technologies become so complex that they surpass individual human understanding. This phenomenon reminds us of the classic novel *Flatland*, in which beings in a two-dimensional world would struggle to conceive of a three-dimensional one.

The deepening integration of increasingly sophisticated AI into our daily lives within the AI-native era will likely amplify its inherent unfathomability. As AI systems evolve towards greater autonomy, adding complex layers to their neural networks will further obscure their internal workings. Tracing the decision-making processes of these advanced algorithms is becoming progressively challenging, with even engineers often struggling to comprehend the rationale behind specific outputs fully. This escalating opacity demands careful consideration, particularly for businesses where AI transparency, robust ethical safeguards, and comprehensive data traceability are becoming critical imperatives. However, individual users constructing their own AI agents may not share the same level of concern for these crucial governance factors, potentially creating a divergence in expectations and risk tolerance.

Given the inherent unpredictability of AI development, a strategic imperative emerges: cultivating organisational agility, adaptability, and the capacity to thrive amidst uncertainty. As futurist Roger Splitz aptly notes, we must learn to "navigate uncharted waters with a compass calibrated for the unpredictable."[5] These capabilities will be foundational for companies aspiring to leadership in the AI-native era. Success will necessitate a deep and early integration of AI into their core structures, fundamental processes, and overarching strategy, not merely as a supplementary add-on. Much like the "mobile-native" companies that outmanoeuvred incumbents by deeply embedding mobile technology rather than simply digitising existing offerings, truly AI-native firms must weave AI into their very fabric, aligning their operations and strategies with the evolving landscape that the technology itself is shaping. This foundational integration will unlock novel efficiencies, create unprecedented opportunities, and ultimately define the competitive vanguard of the AI-native future.

A BRAVE NEW WORLD

Figure 9.1 illustrates the evolution of AI since it garnered the attention of businesses in 2017. In under a decade, the development of artificial intelligence has occurred in distinct phases, transitioning from the Cloud Era to what is now recognised as the AI-native era. This transformation reflects a significant shift in how businesses and individuals interact with technology, with AI evolving from a probabilistic tool focused on prediction to an interactive assistant and, ultimately, a proactive agent capable of autonomous decision-making. The implications of this evolution are considerable, influencing the trajectory of work, business strategy, and personal productivity in ways once considered within the realm of science fiction.

Traditional artificial intelligence, anchored in a rule-based and statistical paradigm, operated like a meticulously organised cookbook. Like a predefined recipe, each algorithm dictated a precise sequence of steps for a specific task, heavily reliant on structured, well-formatted data and probability-driven models for decision-making. A critical limitation, particularly from a business standpoint, was the intricate nature of developing machine learning-powered AI. These initiatives demanded substantial upfront investment in infrastructure and talent, coupled with

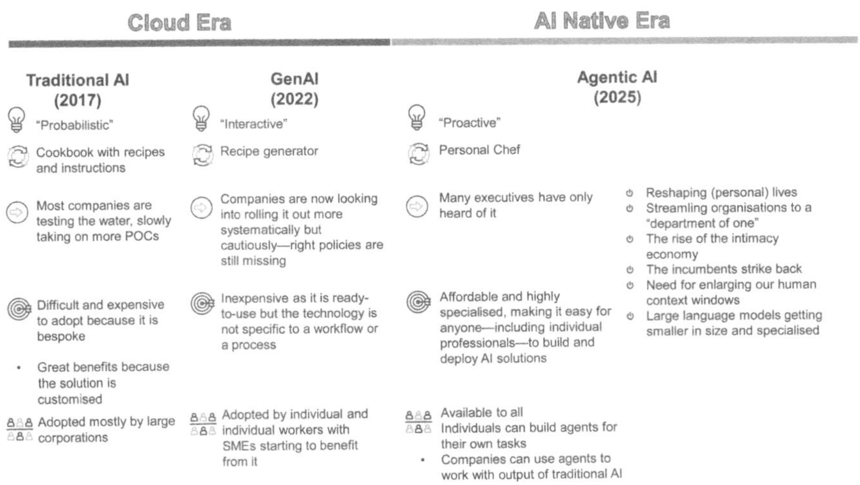

FIGURE 9.1 Evolution of AI from the cloud era to the AI native era.

ongoing, often unpredictable, costs for implementation and maintenance. Furthermore, achieving tangible, business-relevant outcomes necessitated extensive and usually bespoke customisation, tailoring algorithms and models to each organisation's unique data landscape and operational nuances. Consequently, the practical adoption of traditional AI was primarily confined to well-resourced enterprises with the significant financial capacity to absorb these costs and the specialised technical expertise to navigate the complexities of AI development and deployment. This potential was demonstrated by early successes, such as fraud detection systems in large financial institutions like American Express, which leveraged rule-based expert systems to identify anomalous transaction patterns. However, even these pioneers often encountered challenges scaling these initial deployments and realising consistent returns on their considerable investments. Many companies struggled to establish the robust data infrastructure required to feed these AI models effectively, a challenge highlighted by early attempts at predictive maintenance in manufacturing, where inconsistent sensor data often hampered accuracy. Moreover, the scarcity of qualified data scientists and AI engineers proved to be a significant bottleneck. The result was a pervasive trend: numerous organisations progressed only to the proof-of-concept or experimentation phase, often showcasing promising initial results in controlled environments but failing to overcome the hurdles of full-scale implementation across their core operations. This reality cemented the perception of AI as a tool for incremental efficiency improvements, such as automating routine back-office tasks, rather than a strategic lever for fundamental business transformation capable of driving innovation and creating entirely new value propositions. This limitation hampered its broader strategic impact beyond specific, well-defined use cases.

The emergence of GenAI in 2022 marked a pivotal inflexion point, unlocking a spectrum of novel opportunities while simultaneously introducing a fresh set of complexities for businesses to navigate. Unlike its traditional counterpart, which primarily focused on processing existing data to generate predictions or classifications, GenAI introduced interactive and creative capabilities, fundamentally shifting the paradigm from mere analytical processing to the active generation of entirely new content. Instead of rigidly adhering to predefined instructions embedded within its algorithms, GenAI operates more like a versatile recipe generator, capable of synthesising novel outputs and exploring previously unimagined possibilities that extend beyond the confines of its initial training data. This transformative leap has significantly lowered the barriers to AI adoption in two key dimensions. Firstly, GenAI has democratised access to AI capabilities by making them considerably more affordable and readily available. It negates the need for the extensive and costly bespoke customisation that characterised traditional AI deployments. Secondly, GenAI exhibits a remarkable "generalist" aptitude, demonstrating its potential applicability across a broader array of business undertakings, from content creation and marketing to product design and customer service. Nevertheless, targeted fine-tuning remains essential to optimise its performance for specific, granular tasks.

These advancements have democratised AI access beyond the traditional stronghold of large corporations. Small and medium-sized enterprises and even individual professionals have begun to actively explore and experiment with its diverse applications, recognising its potential to enhance productivity and unlock new avenues for innovation. For instance, e-commerce platforms leverage GenAI to generate personalised product descriptions and recommendations, as seen with Amazon's AI-driven suggestion engine, enhancing the customer shopping experience.[6] Marketing teams employ tools like Jasper to rapidly create diverse ad copy and social media content, significantly reducing content creation timelines. Even individual entrepreneurs use GenAI for tasks like drafting business plans and generating initial website content, tasks that previously required significant time or financial investment in external resources. However, despite this increased accessibility and versatility, a palpable hesitancy remains among many business leaders. While executive teams have generally become aware of the GenAI buzz and acknowledge its theoretical potential, they often grapple with a tangible understanding of its broader strategic implications and the profound organisational shifts accompanying its systematic integration across their operations. The potential for large-scale transformation, capable of reshaping entire industries and redefining competitive landscapes, is undeniably evident. Nevertheless, the practical pathways to fully realising the transformative capabilities of GenAI within real-world business contexts remain largely uncharted. Its full impact is currently elusive, requiring further experimentation, strategic vision, and a deeper understanding of its long-term implications, particularly around data quality issues, ethical considerations, and integration with existing infrastructure, as highlighted in recent industry reports.

We now stand at the precipice of the AI native era, a transformative epoch ushered in by the advent of agentic AI. This next stage marks a significant leap beyond interactive assistance towards truly proactive intelligence. Unlike prior generations of AI, which necessitated human prompting and guidance at each step, agentic AI exhibits a nascent form of autonomy, transitioning from a mere provider or generator of new recipes to a personal chef who proactively anticipates needs and executes culinary creations independently. This fundamental shift signifies that AI is no longer relegated to the role of a passive tool that supports human decision-making; it has evolved into an active participant within workflows, capable of independently executing intricate tasks and making complex decisions on behalf of its users, often with minimal direct supervision. A defining characteristic of this agentic AI paradigm is its inherent affordability and increasing specialisation. In stark contrast to traditional AI, which demanded substantial financial investment and extensive, bespoke customisation, and even GenAI, which often requires a degree of tailoring to achieve optimal business utility, agentic AI offers a more cost-effective and readily adaptable solution for specific needs. The emergence of user-friendly platforms and no-code/low-code tools now empowers non-technical professionals to construct and deploy AI-powered solutions, albeit currently focused on relatively straightforward tasks such as automated scheduling, basic data organisation, and routine communication management, without requiring deep coding expertise. Nevertheless, this accessibility represents a watershed moment, democratising AI capabilities and extending its reach far beyond the traditional confines of large corporations with dedicated technical teams. The barriers to entry have been significantly lowered, paving the way for widespread experimentation and integration of intelligent agents across a diverse spectrum of individual and professional endeavours, signalling a fundamental shift in how we interact with and leverage artificial intelligence in our daily lives and business operations.

THE AI NATIVE ERA

This situation requires us to consider the uncertainties ahead. As mentioned earlier, accurately predicting the future of AI is highly speculative. Therefore, our view of what the AI-native era will look like will undoubtedly include some bold assumptions. We are not attempting to be perfect forecasters of social and business trends. Instead, we aim to emphasise the likelihood of significant changes and potential conflicts emerging.

Just as social media and mobile phones have become indispensable, our increasing integration with AI will inevitably reshape our behaviours, customs, and habits, potentially even dictating them. The implications will be profound, impacting everything from financial dealings and political discourse to personal relationships and core values. Simultaneously, as AI's presence and influence within businesses expand, we will witness a continued flattening of organisational hierarchies, potentially leading to scenarios where a single individual can effectively manage an entire department. Businesses that once required extensive teams to oversee operations can now leverage AI to automate significant portions of their workflows, driving down costs, enhancing agility, and fostering a new era of competitive dynamics.

Crucially, as AI becomes more deeply embedded in our personal and professional lives, it will gain an unprecedented understanding of us. Mirroring our relationship with mobile phones and the proliferation of AI-powered applications and agents, we will gradually forge strong dependencies on these technologies for security, convenience, and even a sense of fulfilment—a form of digital intimacy. This intimate understanding will empower businesses to offer hyper-personalised experiences, forging stronger customer relationships than ever before. However, this increasing reliance on AI agents necessitates strategically recalibrating human capabilities. As we delegate and outsource more tasks, we cannot become complacent. Instead, we must cultivate and amplify the uniquely human skills that remain paramount: creativity, advanced problem-solving, and deep, strategic thinking. The future of business will hinge on the symbiotic relationship between human ingenuity and artificial intelligence, not passive delegation. To put it another way, we must expand our human context windows. While AI excels at processing immense datasets and generating insights at speeds far exceeding human capacity, the crucial differentiator lies in our ability to contextualise and interpret these findings effectively. Without this human layer of understanding, businesses risk misinterpreting critical information and falling behind, just as individuals become susceptible to being misled. Those who cultivate the skills to forge genuine human-in-the-loop collaboration with AI will gain a competitive advantage.

The landscape of large language models (LLMs) is also evolving rapidly. The emergence of freely available models, such as those from China, signals a potential shift away from reliance on proprietary systems. LLMs are likely to become more streamlined and specialised in the future. The advantage of these compact models lies in their ability to be precisely tailored to specific business needs, offering enhanced efficiency at reduced costs. This trend will further democratise AI adoption, embedding it more deeply into our daily operations and potentially making generic, large-scale models less indispensable. Therefore, transitioning to an AI-native era represents a profound shift transcending mere technological advancement. It signifies a fundamental redefinition of how businesses and individuals interact with machine intelligence. AI is no longer a supplementary tool; it is becoming integral to strategic decision-making, driving innovation, enhancing operational efficiency, and creating significant competitive advantages. The imperative for businesses is clear: adapt now by embracing AI as an operational asset and a core pillar of future growth and success.

The progression from traditional AI to GenAI and now to Agentic AI underscores the increasing autonomy of artificial intelligence in shaping our world. As organisations and individuals navigate this transformative journey, sustained success will hinge on proactive AI adoption and the cultivation of effective human-AI collaboration. Those who strategically integrate AI into their core strategies and daily operations will spearhead the future, redefining industry landscapes and establishing new benchmarks for what is achievable in the AI era. The implications for the workforce are equally significant. AI-native businesses will inherently require leaner teams to achieve comparable results, catalysing a shift from traditional hierarchical structures toward highly empowered individuals augmented by AI. This transformation will optimise operational efficiency and fundamentally reshape how work is organised and valued, emphasising intellectual agility, strategic oversight, creativity, and ethical judgement as essential competencies.

Furthermore, we face a widening spectrum of ethical challenges. These challenges extend beyond concerns about AI bias, discrimination, or unequal access to automation. We will increasingly grapple with balancing economic imperatives with evolving ethical values, requiring careful consideration as AI's influence deepens. Let's say you are interviewing two candidates, Amy and Betty. Amy has an assessment score of 98, whereas Betty got 95. However, Betty used AI to achieve it, whereas Amy, as it turns out, is not very astute in taking on AI, at least not up to Betty's level. Who would you rather hire?[7] If the former is preferred, should fluency in using AI be valued? If Betty is selected, has she "cheated"? Such fair play versus fraud in terms of AI would seem to be an increasingly common dilemma.

Ultimately, the very fabric of human-machine interaction is poised for a profound transformation in an AI-native environment. Decision-making processes, traditionally the domain of human intellect, will increasingly lean on algorithms that proactively anticipate and execute human intentions, dramatically compressing decision cycles and fundamentally reshaping business agility. The pivotal challenge for organisations will be striking a critical balance: determining the optimal level of autonomy to delegate to agentic AI systems while retaining essential human oversight to safeguard ethical alignment and ensure strategic coherence. This delicate equilibrium will define the future of effective and responsible AI integration in business.

While no definitive forecast can predict every twist and turn in AI's evolution, societies, governments, and businesses retain significant agency in steering its impact. Though the precise future remains uncertain, the advantage will accrue to those who cultivate comfort with ambiguity, proactively implement adaptive governance frameworks, and foster an AI-native culture of agility, curiosity, and unwavering ethical vigilance. Uncertainty may define AI's trajectory, but adaptability, preparedness, and strategic clarity remain firmly within our grasp. Ultimately, the unpredictable future of AI rests not solely in the technology itself but squarely in our hands. This future is unfolding as evidence suggests that the human cognitive peak may have passed, marked by increasing challenges in concentration and declining verbal and numerical reasoning, a crucial context for integrating and leveraging this powerful technology.[8]

Leaders and individuals must ensure we retain core human prerogatives and control rather than inadvertently ceding them to machines. As we navigate the increasing sophistication of AI, particularly agentic systems, a conscious and continuous effort will be required to define the boundaries of delegation. Indeed, even in the context of this book, we, the authors, must remain mindful not to fully outsource the critical thinking, nuanced insight, and creative authorship that define our work to AI agents.

NOTES

1 Kantrowitz, A. (2024) *Can Demis Hassabis save Google?* https://www.bigtechnology.com/p/can-demis-hassabis-save-google. Accessed on 7 March 2025.

2 Fridman, L. (2024) *Sam Altman: OpenAI, GPT-5, Sora, Board Saga, Elon Musk, Ilya, Power & AGI,* https://www.youtube.com/watch?v=jvqFAi7vkBc. Accessed on 29 April 2025.

3 Suddendorf, T., Redshaw, J. and Bulley, A. (2022) *The Invention of Tomorrow: A Natural History of Foresight*. New York: Basic Books.
4 Harari, Y. N. (2024) *Nexus: A Brief History of Information Networks from the Stone Age to AI*. New York: Fern Press.
5 Spitz, R. (2024) *Disrupt with Impact: Achieving Business Success in an Unpredictable World*. London: Kogan Page.
6 Levine, I. (2024) "How Amazon is using generative AI to improve product recommendations and descriptions," https://www.aboutamazon.com/news/retail/amazon-generative-ai-product-search-results-and-descriptions. Accessed on 28 April 2025.
7 The idea of this experiment draws from McRae, E. R. and Lowmaster, K. (2025) *The Gartner Top 9 Future of Work Trends for 2025 and Beyond* [Webinar], https://www.gartner.com/en/webinar/682345/1524481. Accessed on 25 January 2025.
8 Burn-Murdoch, J. (2025) "Have humans passed peak brain power?," https://www.ft.com/content/a8016c64-63b7-458b-a371-e0e1c54a13fc. Accessed on 14 March 2025.

Index

Note: Locators in *italics* represent figures and **bold** indicate tables in the text

B

J

K

L

M

N

O

P

For Product Safety Concerns and Information please contact our EU representative GPSR@taylorandfrancis.com Taylor & Francis Verlag GmbH, Kaufingerstraße 24, 80331 München, Germany